METRIC MEASURE

METRIC IMMERSION:

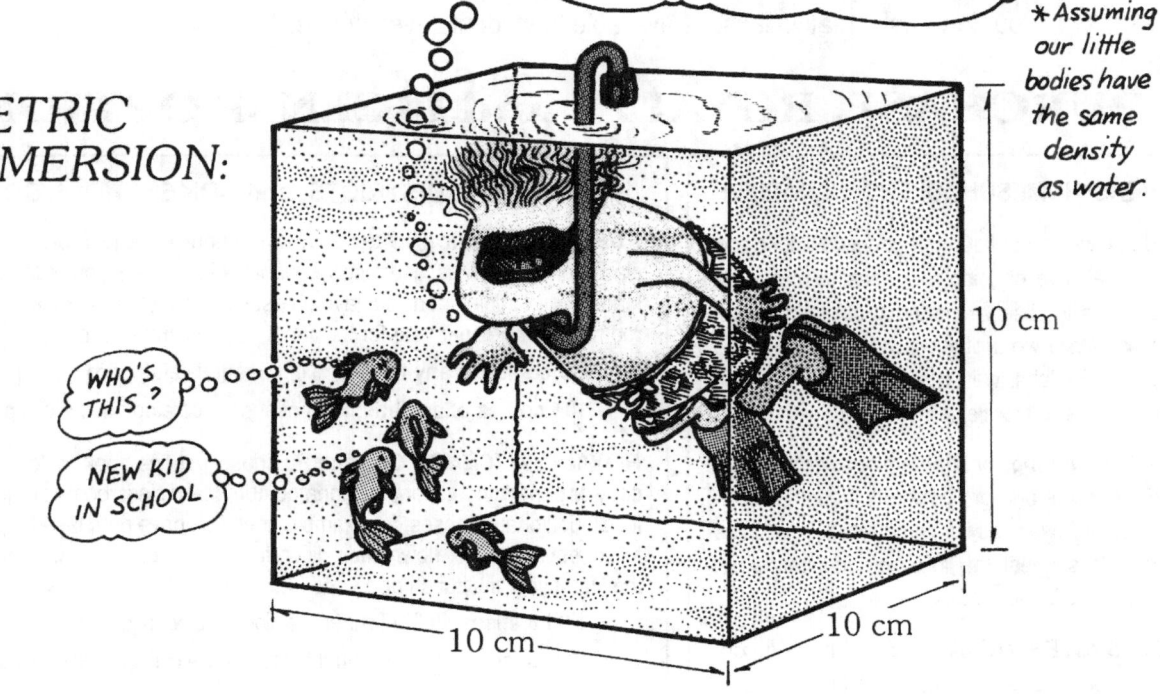

TASK CARD SERIES

Conceived and written by
Ron Marson

Illustrated by
Peg Marson

**342 S Plumas Street
Willows, CA 95988**

www.topscience.org

WHAT CAN YOU COPY?

Dear Educator,

Please honor our copyright restrictions. We offer liberal options and guidelines below with the intention of balancing your needs with ours. When you buy these labs and use them for your own teaching, you sustain our work. If you "loan" or circulate copies to others without compensating TOPS, you squeeze us financially, and make it harder for our small non-profit to survive. Our well-being rests in your hands. Please help us keep our low-cost, creative lessons available to students everywhere. Thank you!

PURCHASE, ROYALTY and LICENSE OPTIONS

TEACHERS, HOMESCHOOLERS, LIBRARIES:

We do all we can to keep our prices low. Like any business, we have ongoing expenses to meet. We trust our users to observe the terms of our copyright restrictions. While we prefer that all users purchase their own TOPS labs, we accept that real-life situations sometimes call for flexibility.

Reselling, trading, or loaning our materials is prohibited unless one or both parties contribute an Honor System Royalty as fair compensation for value received. We suggest the following amounts – let your conscience be your guide.

HONOR SYSTEM ROYALTIES: If making copies from a library, or sharing copies with colleagues, please calculate their value at 50 cents per lesson, or 25 cents for homeschoolers. This contribution may be made at our website or by mail (addresses at the bottom of this page). Any additional tax-deductible contributions to make our ongoing work possible will be accepted gratefully and used well.

Please follow through promptly on your good intentions. Stay legal, and do the right thing.

SCHOOLS, DISTRICTS, and HOMESCHOOL CO-OPS:

PURCHASE Option: Order a book in quantities equal to the number of target classrooms or homes, and receive quantity discounts. If you order 5 books or downloads, for example, then you have unrestricted use of this curriculum for any 5 classrooms or families per year for the life of your institution or co-op.

2-9 copies of any title: 90% of current catalog price + shipping.

10+ copies of any title: 80% of current catalog price + shipping.

ROYALTY/LICENSE Option: Purchase just one book or download *plus* photocopy or printing rights for a designated number of classrooms or families. If you pay for 5 additional Licenses, for example, then you have purchased reproduction rights for an entire book or download edition for any **6** classrooms or families per year for the life of your institution or co-op.

1-9 Licenses: 70% of current catalog price per designated classroom or home.

10+ Licenses: 60% of current catalog price per designated classroom or home.

WORKSHOPS and TEACHER TRAINING PROGRAMS:

We are grateful to all of you who spread the word about TOPS. Please limit copies to only those lessons you will be using, and collect all copyrighted materials afterward. No take-home copies, please. Copies of copies are strictly prohibited.

Copyright © 2000 by TOPS Learning Systems. All rights reserved. This material is created/printed/transmitted in the United States of America. No part of this program may be used, reproduced, or transmitted in any manner whatsoever without written permission from the publisher, *except as explicitly stated above and below*:

The *original owner* of this book or digital download is permitted to make multiple copies of all *student materials* for personal teaching use, provided all reproductions bear copyright notice. A purchasing school or homeschool co-op may assign *one* purchased book or digital download to *one* teacher, classroom, family, or study group *per year*. Reproduction of student materials from libraries is permitted if the user compensates TOPS as outlined above. Reproduction of any copyrighted materials for commercial sale is prohibited.

For licensing, honor system royalty payments, contact: **www.TOPScience.org**; or **TOPS Learning Systems 342 S Plumas St, Willows CA 95988**; or inquire at **customerservice@topscience.org**

ISBN 978-0-941008-76-1

CONTENTS

PART I — INTRODUCTION

  A. A TOPS Model for Effective Science Teaching
  C. Getting Ready
  D. Gathering Materials
  E. Sequencing Task Cards
  F. Long Range Objectives
  G. Review / Test Questions

PART II — TEACHING NOTES

CORE CURRICULUM
1. Decimal Ladder (1)
2. Decimal Ladder (2)
3. Decimal Ladder (3)
4. Length, Area, Volume…
5. Millions and Billions
6. Our Small Speck
7. Sizing Up a Cylinder
8. Liquid Volume
9. Liter Buckets
10. Pouring Grams
11. Mass x Distance
12. Kilos and Pounds
13. Build a Microbalance
14. Millimasses

ENRICHMENT CURRICULUM
15. Pass the Rice
16. Mass Estimate
17. Volume Estimate
18. Area Estimate
19. How Can This Be?
20. Ton of Water

PART III — REPRODUCIBLE STUDENT TASK CARDS

Task Cards 1-20
Supplementary Pages —Centimeter Grid
                      Centimeter Ruler
                      Grid with Inscribed Circle
                      Grid with Millimeter Squares

A TOPS Model for Effective Science Teaching...

If science were only a set of explanations and a collection of facts, you could teach it with blackboard and chalk. You could assign students to read chapters and answer the questions that followed. Good students would take notes, read the text, turn in assignments, then give you all this information back again on a final exam. Science is traditionally taught in this manner. Everybody learns the same body of information at the same time. Class togetherness is preserved.

But science is more than this.

Science is also process — a dynamic interaction of rational inquiry and creative play. Scientists probe, poke, handle, observe, question, think up theories, test ideas, jump to conclusions, make mistakes, revise, synthesize, communicate, disagree and discover. Students can understand science as process only if they are free to think and act like scientists, in a classroom that recognizes and honors individual differences.

Science is *both* a traditional body of knowledge *and* an individualized process of creative inquiry. Science as process cannot ignore tradition. We stand on the shoulders of those who have gone before. If each generation reinvents the wheel, there is no time to discover the stars. Nor can traditional science continue to evolve and redefine itself without process. Science without this cutting edge of discovery is a static, dead thing.

Here is a teaching model that combines the best of both elements into one integrated whole. It is only a model. Like any scientific theory, it must give way over time to new and better ideas. We challenge you to incorporate this TOPS model into your own teaching practice. Change it and make it better so it works for you.

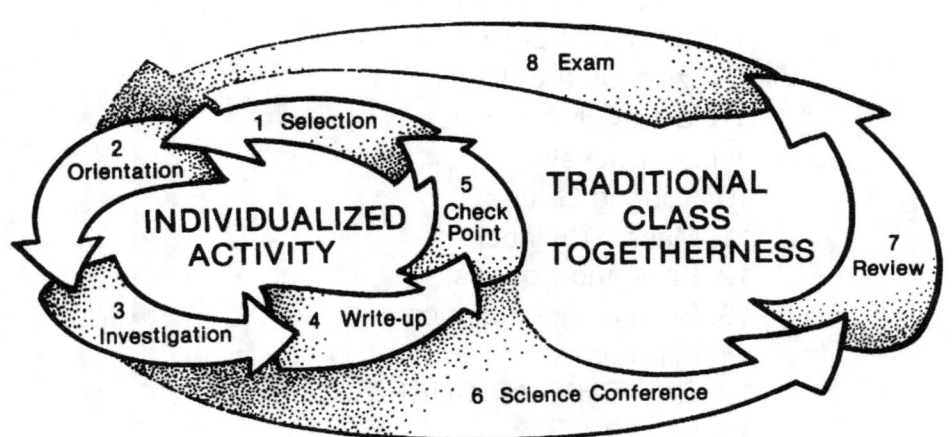

1. SELECTION

Doing TOPS is as easy as selecting the first task card and doing what it says, then the second, then the third, and so on. Working at their own pace, students fall into a natural routine that creates stability and order. They still have questions and problems, to be sure, but students know where they are and where they need to go.

Students generally select task cards in sequence because new concepts build on old ones in a specific order. There are, however, exceptions to this rule: students might *skip* a task that is not challenging; *repeat* a task with doubtful results; *add* a task of their own design to answer original "what would happen if" questions.

2. ORIENTATION

Many students will simply read a task card and immediately understand what to do. Others will require further verbal interpretation. Identify poor readers in your class. When they ask, "What does this mean?" they may be asking in reality, "Will you please read this card aloud?"

With such a diverse range of talent among students, how can you individualize activity and still hope to finish this module as a cohesive group? It's easy. By the time your most advanced students have completed all the task cards, including the enrichment series at the end, your slower students have at least completed the basic core curriculum. This core provides the common background so necessary for meaningful discussion, review and testing on a class basis.

3. INVESTIGATION

Students work through the task cards independently and cooperatively. They follow their own experimental strategies and help each other. You encourage this behavior by helping students only *after* they have tried to help themselves. As a resource person, you work to stay *out* of the center of attention, answering student questions rather than posing teacher questions.

When you need to speak to everyone at once, it is appropriate to interrupt individual task card activity and address the whole class, rather than repeat yourself over and over again. If you plan ahead, you'll find that most interruptions can fit into brief introductory remarks at the beginning of each new period.

4. WRITE-UP

Task cards ask students to explain the "how and why" of things. Write-ups are brief and to the point. Students may accelerate their pace through the task cards by writing these reports out of class.

Students may work alone or in cooperative lab groups. But each one must prepare an original write-up. These must be brought to the teacher for approval as soon as they are completed. Avoid dealing with too many write-ups near the end of the module, by enforcing this simple rule: each write-up must be approved *before* continuing on to the next task card.

5. CHECK POINT

The student and teacher evaluate each write-up together on a pass/no-pass basis. (Thus no time is wasted haggling over grades.) If the student has made reasonable effort consistent with individual ability, the write-up is checked off on a progress chart and included in the student's personal assignment folder or notebook kept on file in class.

Because the student is present when you evaluate, feedback is immediate and effective. A few seconds of this direct student-teacher interaction is surely more effective than 5 minutes worth of margin notes that students may or may not heed. Remember, you don't have to point out every error. Zero in on particulars. If reasonable effort has not been made, direct students to make specific improvements, and see you again for a follow-up check point.

A responsible lab assistant can double the amount of individual attention each student receives. If he or she is mature and respected by your students, have the assistant check the even-numbered write-ups while you check the odd ones. This will balance the work load and insure that all students receive equal treatment.

6. SCIENCE CONFERENCE

After individualized task card activity has ended, this is a time for students to come together, to discuss experimental results, to debate and draw conclusions. Slower students learn about the enrichment activities of faster students. Those who did original investigations, or made unusual discoveries, share this information with their peers, just like scientists at a real conference. This conference is open to films, newspaper articles and community speakers. It is a perfect time to consider the technological and social implications of the topic you are studying.

7. READ AND REVIEW

Does your school have an adopted science textbook? Do parts of your science syllabus still need to be covered? Now is the time to integrate other traditional science resources into your overall program. Your students already share a common background of hands-on lab work. With this shared base of experience, they can now read the text with greater understanding, think and problem-solve more successfully, communicate more effectively.

You might spend just a day on this step or an entire week. Finish with a review of key concepts in preparation for the final exam. Test questions in this module provide an excellent basis for discussion and study.

8. EXAM

Use any combination of the review/test questions, plus questions of your own, to determine how well students have mastered the concepts they've been learning. Those who finish your exam early might begin work on the first activity in the next new TOPS module.

Now that your class has completed a major TOPS learning cycle, it's time to start fresh with a brand new topic. Those who messed up and got behind don't need to stay there. Everyone begins the new topic on an equal footing. This frequent change of pace encourages your students to work hard, to enjoy what they learn, and thereby grow in scientific literacy.

GETTING READY

Here is a checklist of things to think about and preparations to make before your first lesson.

☐ Decide if this TOPS module is the best one to teach next.

TOPS modules are flexible. They can generally be scheduled in any order to meet your own class needs. Some lessons within certain modules, however, do require basic math skills or a knowledge of fundamental laboratory techniques. Review the task cards in this module now if you are not yet familiar with them. Decide whether you should teach any of these other TOPS modules first: *Measuring Length, Graphing, Metric Measure, Weighing* or *Electricity* (before *Magnetism*). It may be that your students already possess these requisite skills or that you can compensate with extra class discussion or special assistance.

☐ Number your task card masters in pencil.

The small number printed in the lower right corner of each task card shows its position within the overall series. If this ordering fits your schedule, copy each number into the blank parentheses directly above it at the top of the card. Be sure to use pencil rather than ink. You may decide to revise, upgrade or rearrange these task cards next time you teach this module. To do this, write your own better ideas on blank 4 x 6 index cards, and renumber them into the task card sequence wherever they fit best. In this manner, your curriculum will adapt and grow as you do.

☐ Copy your task card masters.

You have our permission to reproduce these task cards, for as long as you teach, with only 1 restriction: please limit the distribution of copies you make to the students you personally teach. Encourage other teachers who want to use this module to purchase their *own* copy. This supports TOPS financially, enabling us to continue publishing new TOPS modules for you. For a full list of task card options, please turn to the first task card masters numbered "cards 1-2."

☐ Collect needed materials.

Please see the opposite page.

☐ Organize a way to track completed assignment.

Keep write-ups on file in class. If you lack a vertical file, a box with a brick will serve. File folders or notebooks both make suitable assignment organizers. Students will feel a sense of accomplishment as they see their file folders grow heavy, or their notebooks fill up, with completed assignments. Easy reference and convenient review are assured, since all papers remain in one place.

Ask students to staple a sheet of numbered graph paper to the inside front cover of their file folder or notebook. Use this paper to track each student's progress through the module. Simply initial the corresponding task card number as students turn in each assignment.

☐ Review safety procedures.

Most TOPS experiments are safe even for small children. Certain lessons, however, require heat from a candle flame or Bunsen burner. Others require students to handle sharp objects like scissors, straight pins and razor blades. These task cards should not be attempted by immature students unless they are closely supervised. You might choose instead to turn these experiments into teacher demonstrations.

Unusual hazards are noted in the teaching notes and task cards where appropriate. But the curriculum cannot anticipate irresponsible behavior or negligence. It is ultimately the teacher's responsibility to see that common sense safety rules are followed at all times. Begin with these basic safety rules:
1. Eye Protection: Wear safety goggles when heating liquids or solids to high temperatures.
2. Poisons: Never taste anything unless told to do so.
3. Fire: Keep loose hair or clothing away from flames. Point test tubes which are heating away from your face and your neighbor's.
4. Glass Tubing: Don't force through stoppers. (The teacher should fit glass tubes to stoppers in advance, using a lubricant.)
5. Gas: Light the match first, before turning on the gas.

☐ Communicate your grading expectations.

Whatever your philosophy of grading, your students need to understand the standards you expect and how they will be assessed. Here is a grading scheme that counts individual effort, attitude and overall achievement. We think these 3 components deserve equal weight:

1. Pace (effort): Tally the number of check points you have initialed on the graph paper attached to each student's file folder or science notebook. Low ability students should be able to keep pace with gifted students, since write-ups are evaluated relative to individual performance standards. Students with absences or those who tend to work at a slow pace may (or may not) choose to overcome this disadvantage by assigning themselves more homework out of class.

2. Participation (attitude): This is a subjective grade assigned to reflect each student's attitude and class behavior. Active participators who work to capacity receive high marks. Inactive onlookers, who waste time in class and copy the results of others, receive low marks.

3. Exam (achievement): Task cards point toward generalizations that provide a base for hypothesizing and predicting. A final test over the entire module determines whether students understand relevant theory and can apply it in a predictive way.

Gathering Materials

Listed below is everything you'll need to teach this module. You already have many of these items. The rest are available from your supermarket, drugstore and hardware store. Laboratory supplies may be ordered through a science supply catalog. Hobby stores also carry basic science equipment.

Keep this classification key in mind as you review what's needed:

special in-a-box materials:	general on-the-shelf materials:
Italic type suggests that these materials are unusual. Keep these specialty items in a separate box. After you finish teaching this module, label the box for storage and put it away, ready to use again the next time you teach this module.	Normal type suggests that these materials are common. Keep these basics on shelves or in drawers that are readily accessible to your students. The next TOPS module you teach will likely utilize many of these same materials.
(substituted materials):	*optional materials:
Parentheses enclosing any item suggests a ready substitute. These alternatives may work just as well as the original, perhaps better. Don't be afraid to improvise, to make do with what you have.	An asterisk sets these items apart. They are nice to have, but you can easily live without them. They are probably not worth the extra trip, unless you are gathering other materials as well.

Everything is listed in order of first use. Start gathering at the top of this list and work down. Ask students to bring recycled items from home. The teaching notes may occasionally suggest additional student activity under the heading "Extensions." Materials for these optional experiments are listed neither here nor in the teaching notes. Read the extension itself to find out what new materials, if any, are required.

Needed quantities depend on how many students you have, how you organize them into activity groups, and how you teach. Decide which of these 3 estimates best applies to you, then adjust quantities up or down as necessary:

$Q_1 / Q_2 / Q_3$
- **Single Student:** Enough for 1 student to do all the experiments.
- **Individualized Approach:** Enough for 30 students informally working in 10 lab groups, all self-paced.
- **Traditional Approach:** Enough for 30 students, organized into 10 lab groups, all doing the same lesson.

KEY:	*special in-a-box materials* (substituted materials)	general on-the-shelf materials *optional materials

$Q_1 / Q_2 / Q_3$

1/10/10	*calculators		3/30/30	straight straws
1/10/10	scissors		1/10/10	paper clips
1/5/10	rolls cellophane tape		1/10/10	test tubes
4/40/40	meters kite string		1/10/10	*tall beverage bottles — quart or 2 liter size*
1/10/10	meter sticks		1/10/10	plastic produce bags
1/10/10	pinches table salt		1/10/10	plastic sandwich bags (produce bags)
1/4/10	hand lenses		1/10/10	*liters gravel or sand*
1/10/10	straight pins		1/5/10	1 pound bag of long-grained white rice — see notes 12
1/10/10	empty cans – see notes 7			
1/10/10	eyedroppers		1/10/10	clothespins
1/5/10	rolls masking tape		1/1/1	spool thread
1/10/10	10 ml graduated cylinders		1/10/10	paper cups
1/1/1	source of water		1/10/10	*bills, US or Canadian, $1 or higher*
1/10/10	100 ml graduated cylinders		1/10/10	baby food jars with lids
1/4/10	*pie tins or plates		1/1/1	roll paper towels
2/20/20	*half-gallon milk cartons*		1/5/10	index cards
1/2/5	paper punches		1/10/10	*full sheets of newspaper*

Sequencing Task Cards

This logic tree shows how all the task cards in this module tie together. In general, students begin at the trunk of the tree and work up through the related branches. As the diagram suggests, the way to upper level activities leads up from lower level activities.

At the teacher's discretion, certain activities can be omitted or sequences changed to meet specific class needs. The only activities that must be completed in sequence are indicated by leaves that open *vertically* into the ones above them. In these cases the lower activity is a prerequisite to the upper.

When possible, students should complete the task cards in the same sequence as numbered. If time is short, however, or certain students need to catch up, you can use the logic tree to identify concept-related *horizontal* activities. Some of these might be omitted since they serve only to reinforce learned concepts rather than introduce new ones.

On the other hand, if students complete all the activities at a certain horizontal concept level, then experience difficulty at the next higher level, you might go back down the logic tree to have students repeat specific key activities for greater reinforcement.

For whatever reason, when you wish to make sequence changes, you'll find this logic tree a valuable reference. Parentheses in the upper right corner of each task card allow you total flexibility. They are left blank so you can pencil in sequence numbers of your own choosing.

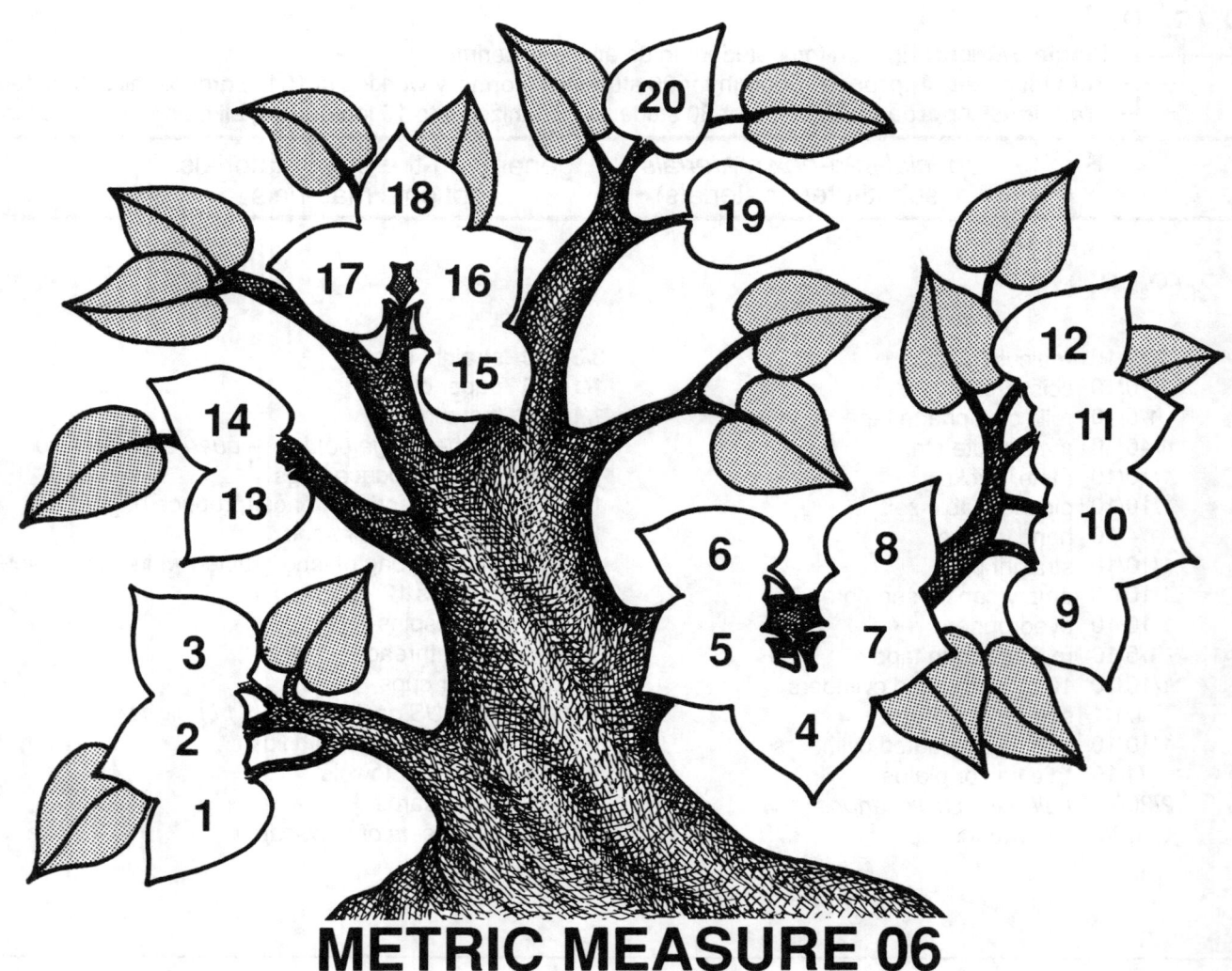

METRIC MEASURE 06

LONG-RANGE OBJECTIVES

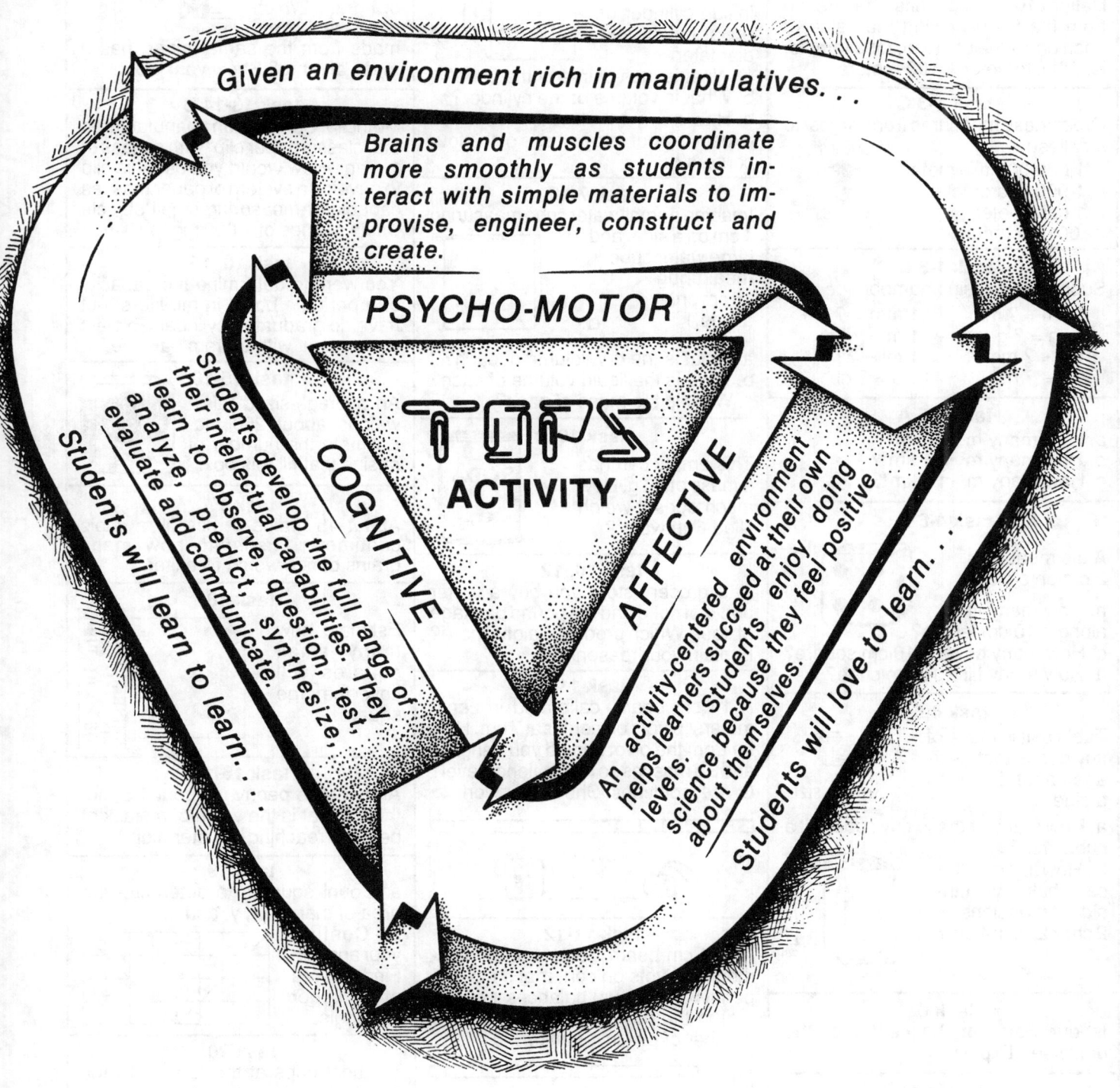

Review / Test Questions

Photocopy the questions below. On a separate sheet of blank paper, cut and paste those boxes you want to use as test questions. Include questions of your own design, as well. Crowd all these questions onto a single page for students to answer on another paper, or leave space for student responses after each question, as you wish. Duplicate a class set and your custom-made test is ready to use. Use leftover questions as a review in preparation for the final exam.

task 1-3 A
How many million are in a billion?

task 1-3 B
Define 10 metric units that derive from the meter, giving the value of each one. One of these, for example, is: 1 hectometer = 100 meters.

task 1-3 C
Order these measures from largest to smallest: LARGEST ↕ SMALLEST
1,000,000 millimeter
1,000 micrometer
1 centimeter
.001 kilometer

task 1-3 D
Supply the missing number.
1 cm = ? mm   1 mm = ? cm
1 kg = ? g   1 m = ? km
1 g = ? mg   1 ml = ? l
1 s = ? ns   1 b = ? gb

task 4-6 A
a. How many m in 1 km?
b. How many m² in 1 km²?
c. How many m³ in 1 km³?

task 4-6 B

A die measures 2 cm on a side.
a. How many fit along a 10 cm length?
c. How many cover a 10 cm square?
a. How many fill a 10 cm cube?

task 4-6 C
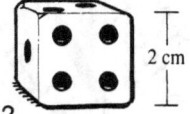
Table salt is made of tiny cubes that average about .5 mm on a side. (10 x ACTUAL SIZE)
a. How many of these tiny cubes fill a cubic mm?
b. How many fill a salt shaker with inside dimensions of 2 cm x 2 cm x 4 cm?

task 6
Is our Earth at the center of the universe? Explain.

task 7-9
A pipe has a cross-sectional opening of 4 cm². What length of pipe will hold a liter of water?

task 7-8
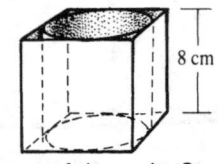
An open cube measuring 8 cm on a side holds an inside cylinder of equal height and diameter.
a. What is the volume of the cube?
b. What is volume of the cylinder?
c. How many ml of water could you expect to pour into just one of the four corners?

task 7-10
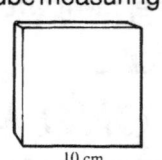
Imagine a small water cube measuring 1 cm on a side, and a large water cube measuring 10 cm on a side.
a. What is the dry volume of each?
b. What is the liquid volume of each?
c. What is the mass of each?

task 10

This empty can has a mass of 16 g. How much does it weigh filled with water? SODA 354 ml

task 10, 12
At a grocery store you buy a 2 liter bottle of coke and a 5 pound package of flour. Which product weighs more? Explain your reasoning.

task 11
A 14 cm beam, calibrated in centimeters, pivots on center at 7 cm. How far from the pivot should you hang 2 g and 3 g masses so they balance level? Give 2 solutions. Show your work.
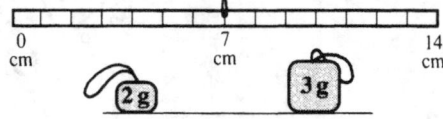

task 11-12
An 18 cm beam, calibrated in centimeters, pivots on center at 9 cm. If 5 pennyweight (pwt) balances 1 ounce (oz) in the positions shown, find the number of pwt in 1 ounce.
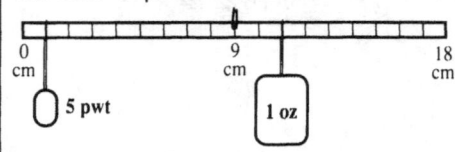

task 13-14 A
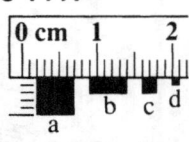
A 10 by 10 cm square of black paper has a mass of 1 gram. Which of these boxes, made from the same paper, has a mass of 1 mg? Show your work.

task 13-14 B
Metriclip Corporation manufactures the "classic paper clip" with a mass of 1 gram. How would you use this clip to develop a system of paper masses capable of measuring small objects within a range of 1,000 mg to 10 mg?

task 10, 15
You want to determine the capacity of a perfume bottle in milliliters, but have no graduated cylinder. Explain how to do it with a gram balance.

task 15-16
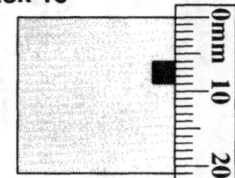
An average-sized raisin weighs about 250 mg. Estimate the number of raisins that fill this box. wrinkle's raisins 425 g

task 17
About 45 grains of rice fill a cubic centimeter. Estimate how many grains of rice would fill a liter.

task 18

Estimate how many small squares will cover the large square.

task 16-18
An average penny is about 1.5 mm thick. What is the value of a stack of pennies reaching 1 meter high?

task 19
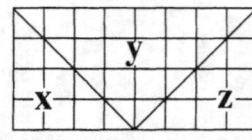
a. Count squares to determine the area of triangle x, y, and z.
b. Confirm your answer. Find the area of the larger rectangle.

task 20
A faucet drips at the rate of 10 ml/minute. How much time passes before the dripping faucet wastes...
a. 1 liter of water?
b. 1 metric ton of water?

Copyright © 1992 by TOPS Learning Systems.

Answers

task 1-3 A
1,000 (1,000,000) = 1,000,000,000
Thus, 1,000 million = 1 billion

task 1-3 B
1 gigameter = 10^9 meters
1 megameter = 10^6 meters
1 kilometer = 10^3 meters
1 hectometer = 100 meters
1 dekameter = 10 meters
(1 meter = 1 meter)
1 decimeter = .1 meters
1 centimeter = .01 meters
1 millimeter = 10^{-3} meters
1 micrometer = 10^{-6} meters
1 nanometer = 10^{-9} meters

task 1-3 C
(LARGEST)
1,000,000 millimeters (1 km)
.001 kilometer (1 m)
1 centimeter
1,000 micrometers (1 mm)
(SMALLEST)

task 1-3 D
1 cm = 10 mm   1 mm = .1 cm
1 kg = 1,000 g   1 m = .001 km
1 g = 1,000 mg   1 ml = .001 l
1 s = 10^9 ns 1 b = 10^{-9} gb

task 4-6 A
a. 1 km = 10^3 m
b. 1 km^2 = 10^3 m × 10^3 m = 10^6 m^2
c. 1 km^3 = 10^3 m × 10^3 m × 10^3 m
    = 10^9 m^3

task 4-6 B
a. 5 dice
b. 25 dice (5 × 5)
c. 125 dice (5 × 5 × 5)

task 4-6 C
a. Two salt cubes fit into the side of a cubic mm cube. Thus 8 salt cubes (2 × 2 × 2) fill the volume.
b. $V_{salt\ shaker}$ = 20 mm × 20 mm × 40 mm
    = 16,000 mm^3
    16,000 mm^3 × $\frac{8\ salt\ cubes}{mm^3}$
    = 128,000 salt cubes

task 6
No. Our Earth is located in an outer arm of our home Milky Way Galaxy revolving around 1 of its 200 billion stars we call the sun. The Milky Way is just one of an estimated 100 billion galaxies flung across the universe.

task 7-9
1 liter = 1,000 ml = 1,000 cm^3
1,000 cm^3 × $\frac{1}{4\ cm^2}$ = 250 cm of pipe

task 7-8
a. V_{cube} = 8 cm × 8 cm × 8 cm
   = 512 cm^3
b. A_{top} = πr^2 = (3.14)(4)^2
   = 50.2 cm^2
   V_{cyl} = Ah = 50.2 cm^2 × 8 cm
   = 402 cm^3
c. $V_{4\ cor}$ = 512 cm^3 – 402 cm^3
   = 110 cm^3
   $V_{1\ cor}$ = $\frac{110\ cm^3}{4}$ = 27.5 cm^3

task 7-10
a. V_{small} = 1 cm × 1 cm × 1 cm
      = 1 cm^3
   V_{large} = 10 cm × 10 cm × 10 cm
      = 1,000 cm^3
b. V_{small} = 1 ml
   V_{large} = 1 l
c. M_{small} = 1 g
   M_{large} = 1 kg

task 10
354 ml water = 354 g
mass of can = 16 g
                370 g

task 10, 12
Coke has about the same density as water:
2 liter × $\frac{1\ kg}{1\ liter}$ × $\frac{2.2\ lb}{1\ kg}$ = 4.4 lb
It weighs slightly less than the 5 lb package of flour.

task 11
Hang the 2 g mass 3 cm from the pivot, and the 3 g mass 2 cm away.
(2 g)(3 cm) = (3 g)(2 cm)
Or hang the 2 g mass 6 cm from the pivot and the 3 g mass 4 cm away.
(2 g)(6 cm) = (3 g)(4 cm)

task 11-12
(1 oz)(2 cm) = (5 pwt)(8 cm)
1 oz = 5 pwt (4) = 20 pwt

task 13-14 A
1 gram = 100 cm^2
$\frac{1\ gram}{1000}$ = $\frac{100\ cm^2}{1000}$
1 mg = .1 cm^2
Area b = (.5 cm)(.2 cm) = .1 cm^2

task 13-14 B
Place the 1 gram "classic clip" on one side of a centered balance, with just enough paper on the other side to rebalance the beam. Then cut, fold and label a 500 mg mass using *half* this paper; make two 200 mg masses using a *fifth* of this paper, etc. Proceed in this manner until you develop this series: 1,000 mg (classic clip), 500 mg, 200 mg, 200 mg, 100 mg, 50 mg, 20 mg, 20 mg, 10 mg.

task 10, 15
Find the mass of the perfume bottle both empty and filled with water. The difference between these masses in grams is the liquid capacity of the perfume bottle in milliliters.

task 15-16
425 g × $\frac{1,000\ mg}{1\ g}$ × $\frac{1\ raisin}{250\ mg}$
   = 1,700 raisins

task 17
1 liter × $\frac{1,000\ cm^3}{1\ liter}$ × $\frac{45\ grains\ rice}{cm^3}$
   = 45,000 grains

task 18
$A_{lg\ sq}$ = 21 mm × 21 mm = 441 mm^2
$V_{sm\ sq}$ = 3 mm × 3 mm = 9 mm^2
Divide the area of the small square into the area of the large square to find how many times it fits:
$\frac{441\ mm^2}{9\ mm^2}$ = 49 times

task 16-18
1 m × $\frac{1,000\ mm}{1\ m}$ × $\frac{\$.01}{1.5\ mm}$ = $6.67

task 19
a. Δx = 8 squares
   Δy = 16 squares
   Δz = 8 squares
b. The sum of the Δs is 32 squares. This is confirmed by the area of the large rectangle: A = 8 × 4 = 32 squares.

task 20
a. 1 liter × $\frac{1,000\ ml}{l\ liter}$ × $\frac{1\ min}{10\ ml}$
   = 100 min
b. 1 ton × $\frac{1\ m^3}{1\ ton}$ × $\frac{1,000\ l}{1\ m^3}$ × $\frac{100\ min}{1\ l}$
   = 10^5 min
100,000 min × $\frac{1\ hr}{60\ min}$ × $\frac{1\ day}{24\ hrs}$
   = 69 days

TEACHING NOTES
For Activities 1-20

Task Objective (TO) practice using numeral place values as language, powers of ten, and decimal numbers.

DECIMAL LADDER (1)

1. Write this equation on the middle line of a sheet of notebook paper, to the right of the margin line: **one = 10^0 = 1.**
2. Follow this pattern *upward*, writing equations 1 line at a time, until you reach a billion.
3. Start again at "one" and go *down* until you reach a billionth.

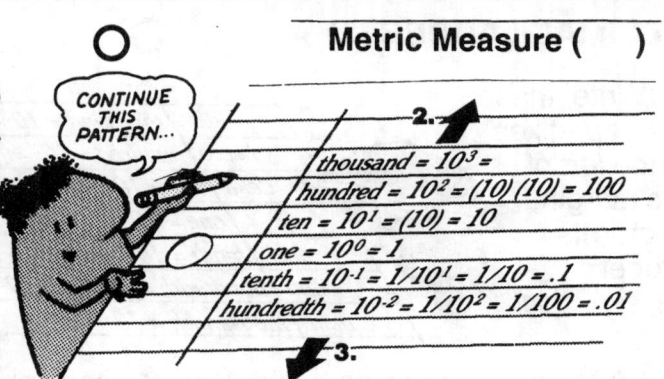

4. Think of the lines on notebook paper as rungs on a ladder.

a. These equations are *one* rung apart. Balance them:
(?) ten = hundred
(?) thousand = hundred
(?) hundredth = tenth
(?) one = tenth

b. These equations are *three* rungs apart. Balance them:
(?) ten = ten thousand
(?) hundredth = ten
(?) one = thousandth
(?) thousandth = millionth

c. How do you balance equations between larger and smaller numbers on this decimal ladder? Invent a rule.

© 1992 by TOPS Learning Systems

Answers / Notes

1-3. *Insist on accuracy and neatness in this important exercise. Metric measurement and decimals are two sides of the same conceptual coin.*

billion = 10^9 = (10)(10)(10)(10)(10)(10)(10)(10)(10) = 1,000,000,000
hundred million = 10^8 = (10)(10)(10)(10)(10)(10)(10)(10) = 100,000,000
ten million = 10^7 = (10)(10)(10)(10)(10)(10)(10) = 10,000,000
million = 10^6 = (10)(10)(10)(10)(10)(10) = 1,000,000
hundred thousand = 10^5 = (10)(10)(10)(10)(10) = 100,000
ten thousand = 10^4 = (10)(10)(10)(10) = 10,000
thousand = 10^3 = (10)(10)(10) = 1,000
hundred = 10^2 = (10)(10) = 100
ten = 10^1 = (10) = 10
one = 10^0 = 1
tenth = 10^{-1} = $1/10^1$ = 1/10 = .1
hundredth = 10^{-2} = $1/10^2$ = 1/100 = .01
thousandth = 10^{-3} = $1/10^3$ = 1/1,000 = .001
ten thousandth = 10^{-4} = $1/10^4$ = 1/10,000 = .0001
hundred thousandth = 10^{-5} = $1/10^5$ = 1/100,000 = .00001
millionth = 10^{-6} = $1/10^6$ = 1/1,000,000 = .000001
ten millionth = 10^{-7} = $1/10^7$ = 1/10,000,000 = .0000001
hundred millionth = 10^{-8} = $1/10^8$ = 1/100,000,000 = .00000001
billionth = 10^{-9} = $1/10^9$ = 1/1,000,000,000 = .000000001

4a. (10)(ten) = hundred
(.1)(thousand) = hundred
(10)(hundredth) = tenth
(.1)(one) = tenth

4b. (1000)(ten) = ten thousand
(1000)(hundredth) = ten
(.001)(one) = thousandth
(.001)(thousandth) = millionth

4c. To balance equations between larger and smaller numbers, simply multiply the smaller or divide the larger by a power of 10 equal to the number of rungs that separate them.

Materials

☐ Notebook paper.

(TO) define metric prefixes in terms of the decimal ladder. To practice translating these prefixes to their numerical equivalents.

DECIMAL LADDER (2)   Metric Measure (   )

1. Write these metric prefixes to the *left* of the margin, each in its proper place:

kilo	thousand = 10^3 =
hecto	hundred = 10^2 = (1
deka	ten = 10^1 = (10) = 10
	one = 10^0 = 1
deci	tenth = 10^{-1} = $1/10^1$ = 1/
centi	hundredth = 10^{-2} = $1/10^2$ =
milli	thousandth = 10^{-3} =

2. Include these additional prefixes higher and lower on your ladder:

giga = billion,
mega = million;
micro = millionth;
nano = billionth.

3. Write the *number* equivalent of a: kiloelephant, millipickle, dekarabbit, decidollar, centidollar, megafish, gigastar, nanopart, hectostudent, micropie.

4. Write the *metric* equivalent of: 100 seconds; .1 bushels; a million volts; .001 ounce; 10^{-6} second; 10 inches; 10^9 watts; .01 miles; a billionth gram; 1,000 years.

5. Use your decimal ladder to solve each problem. Explain your reasoning.
   a. Have you ever run a million millimeters? How far is it?
   b. Would you rather have a gigacent or a megadollar?
   c. Can you hold your breath for a kilosecond?
   d. Have you ever slept a milliyear without waking up?

© 1992 by TOPS Learning Systems

Answers / Notes

1-2.

giga	billion
	hundred million
	ten million
mega	million
	hundred thousand
	ten thousand
kilo	thousand
hecto	hundred
deka	ten
	one
deci	tenth
centi	hundredth
milli	thousandth
	ten thousandth
	hundred thousandth
micro	millionth
	ten millionth
	hundred millionth
nano	billionth

3. kiloelephant = 1,000 elephants
millipickle = .001 pickles
dekarabbit = 10 rabbits
decidollar = .1 dollars = 1 dime
centidollar = .01 dollars = 1 penny
megafish = 10^6 fish or 1,000,000 fish
gigastar = 10^9 stars or 1,000,000,000 stars
nanopart = 10^{-9} parts or .000000001 parts
hectostudent = 100 students
micropie = 10^{-6} pies or .000001 pies

5a. Yes. 1,000,000 millimeters = 1,000 meters = 1 kilometer.

5b. A gigacent has ten times more value than a megadollar:
gigacent = 10^9 cents = 10^7 dollars
megadollar = 10^6 dollars

5c. No: 1 kilosecond = 1,000 seconds

$$1{,}000 \text{ seconds} \times \frac{1 \text{ min}}{60 \text{ sec}} = 16.7 \text{ minutes}$$

5d. Yes: 1 milliyear = .001 years

$$.001 \text{ years} \times \frac{365 \text{ days}}{1 \text{ year}} \times \frac{24 \text{ hours}}{1 \text{ day}} = 8.8 \text{ hours}$$

4. hectosecond
decibushel
megavolt
milliounce
microsecond
dekainch
gigawatt
centimile
nanogram
kiloyear

Materials

☐ The decimal ladder from activity 1.
☐ A calculator (optional).

(TO) practice converting common forms of metric units. To understand and use metric abbreviations.

DECIMAL LADDER (3)   Metric Measure (   )

1. Write 2 balanced equations for each set of measures. The first one is worked as an example.
   a. centimeters (cm) / millimeters (mm)
   b. kilometers (km) / meters (m)
   c. meters / millimeters (mm)
   d. kilograms (kg) / grams (g)
   e. grams / milligrams (mg)
   f. liters (l) / milliliters (ml)
   g. seconds (s) / microseconds (mcs)
   h. seconds / nanoseconds (ns)
   i. megabytes (mgb) / bytes (b)
   j. gigabytes (gb) / bytes

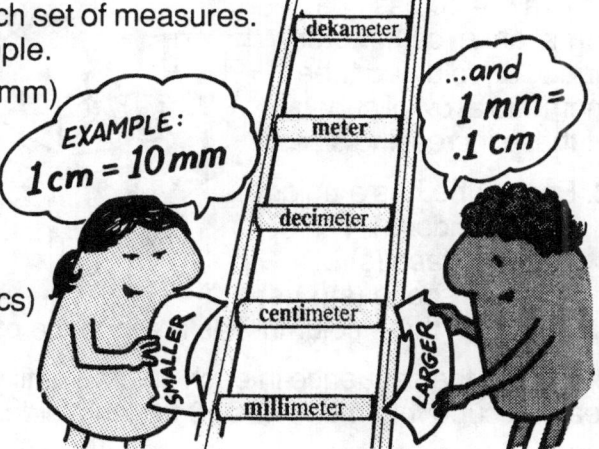

EXAMPLE: 1 cm = 10 mm ...and 1 mm = .1 cm

2. Write two more balanced equations for each of these pairs of English units:
   a. feet / inches   b. pounds / ounces

3. Units are interchangeable in both the metric system and English system. Which system is easier to use? Why?

© 1992 by TOPS Learning Systems

Answers / Notes

1. a. 1 cm = 10 mm
      .1 cm = 1 mm
   b. 1 km = 1,000 m
      .001 km = 1 m
   c. 1 m = 1,000 mm
      .001 m = 1 mm
   d. 1 kg = 1,000 g
      .001 kg = 1 g
   e. 1 g = 1,000 mg
      .001 g = 1 mg
   f. 1 l = 1000 ml
      .001 l = 1 ml
   g. 1 s = 10^6 mcs
      10^{-6} s = 1 mcs
   h. 1 s = 10^9 ns
      10^{-9} s = 1 ns
   i. 1 mgb = 10^6 b
      10^{-6} mgb = 1 b
   j. 1 gb = 10^9 b
      10^{-9} gb = 1 b

2. a. 1 foot = 12 inches
      .083 feet = 1 inch
   b. 1 pound = 16 ounces
      .0625 pounds = 1 ounce

3. The metric system is easier to use. All units in this system are related to each other by multiples of 10. Converting from one unit to another is simply a matter of moving the decimal point right (multiplying) or left (dividing).

Materials
☐ The decimal ladder from activity 1.
☐ A calculator (optional).

(TO) relate increases in length, area and volume to growth in one, two and three dimensions.

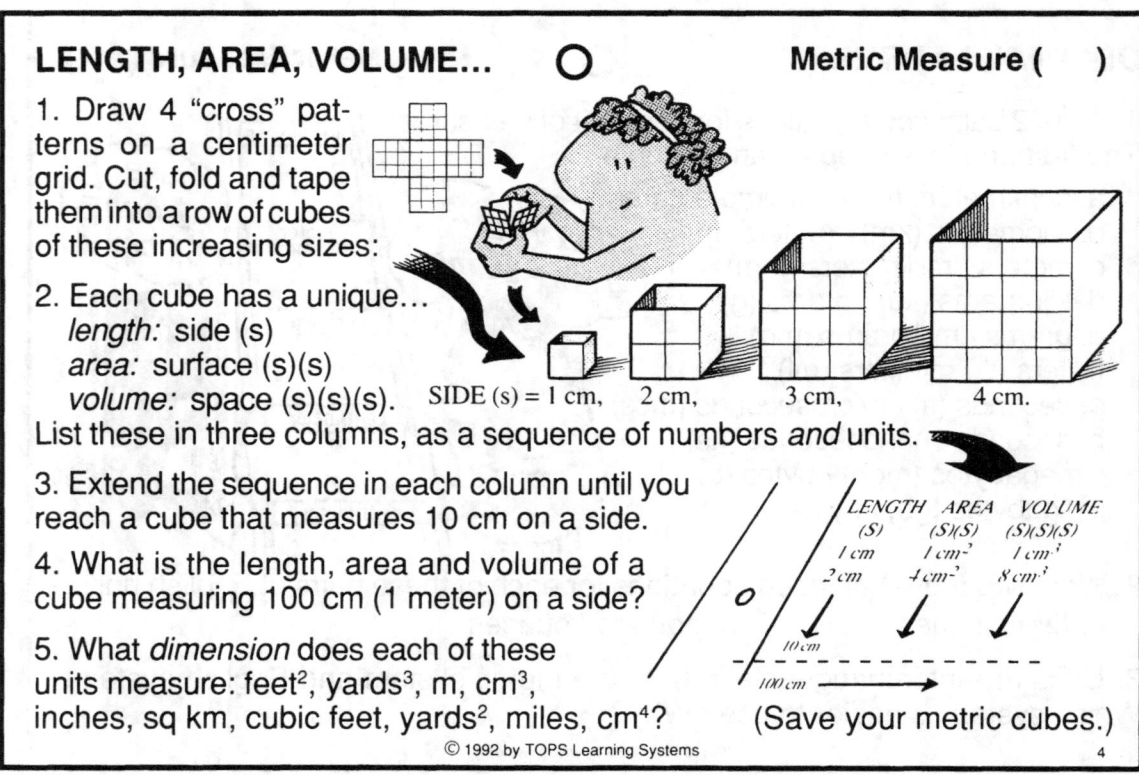

LENGTH, AREA, VOLUME... ○   Metric Measure ( )

1. Draw 4 "cross" patterns on a centimeter grid. Cut, fold and tape them into a row of cubes of these increasing sizes:

2. Each cube has a unique...
   length: side (s)
   area: surface (s)(s)
   volume: space (s)(s)(s).   SIDE (s) = 1 cm, 2 cm, 3 cm, 4 cm.
   List these in three columns, as a sequence of numbers *and* units.

3. Extend the sequence in each column until you reach a cube that measures 10 cm on a side.

4. What is the length, area and volume of a cube measuring 100 cm (1 meter) on a side?

5. What *dimension* does each of these units measure: feet^2, yards^3, m, cm^3, inches, sq km, cubic feet, yards^2, miles, cm^4?

© 1992 by TOPS Learning Systems

(Save your metric cubes.)

4

Answers / Notes

1. *To create each cross-shaped pattern, draw a central square with the proper number of centimeters on a side (1 cm, 2 cm, 3 cm, and 4 cm respectively). Trace 4 additional squares of the same size around this central square to complete each pattern. Cut, fold and tape these patterns into open boxes.*
   Conserve tape by using small pieces.

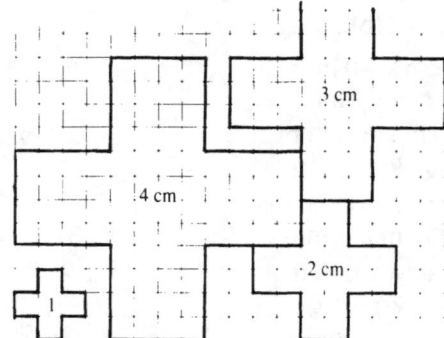

2-4.
LENGTH (S)	AREA (S)(S)	VOLUME (S)(S)(S)
1 cm	1 cm^2	1 cm^3
2 cm	2 cm^2	8 cm^3
3 cm	9 cm^2	27 cm^3
4 cm	16 cm^2	64 cm^3
5 cm	25 cm^2	125 cm^3
6 cm	36 cm^2	216 cm^3
7 cm	49 cm^2	343 cm^3
8 cm	64 cm^2	512 cm^3
9 cm	81 cm^2	729 cm^3
10 cm	100 cm^2	1,000 cm^3
100 cm	10,000 cm^2	1,000,000 cm^3 ← metric cube

5. Length: m, inches, miles
   Area: feet^2, sq km, yards^2
   Volume: yards^3, cm^3, cubic feet
   4th Dimension: cm^4
   Four dimensions, and beyond, are much easier to define mathematically than to comprehend physically. This last unit, centimeters to the 4th power, is added to bend the mind and stretch the imagination.

Materials

☐ A centimeter grid. Photocopy this from the supplementary sheet at the back of this book. With planning, one grid per student is sufficient to make all 4 cubes.
☐ Scissors.
☐ Cellophane tape.
☐ Notebook paper.

(TO) model cubic meters, cubic centimeters and cubic millimeters. To comprehend the size of a million and billion in terms of these models.

MILLIONS AND BILLIONS ○   **Metric Measure (   )**

1. Cut 3 pieces of string that each measure one meter.

2. Tape them to your largest (4 cm³) cube, so each string extends outward in a different dimension from the same corner.

3. Set your cube on the floor. Extend its strings at right angles, either holding the vertical string or taping it to something.

   a. Put your smallest cm cube into the largest one where the strings meet. How many of these small cm cubes fill a metric cube? Explain your reasoning.

   b. Does your answer agree with the previous activity? Explain.

4. A cube measuring 1 x 1 x 1 mm is no bigger than this:  ACTUAL SIZE

   a. How many mm cubes fill a cm cube? Show your work.
   b. How many mm cubes fill a m cube? Show your work.

© 1992 by TOPS Learning Systems

Introduction
There are many different ways to describe a centimeter cube. They all say the same thing:
- 1 centimeter cube
- 1 cubic centimeter
- 1 x 1 x 1 cm cube
- 1 cm³

ACTUAL SIZE

Review these interchangeable terms, then apply them to a larger cubic meter and a tiny cubic millimeter.

Answers / Notes

3. *A meter stick taped to a table or chair provides an ideal support for the vertical string. An empty room corner can also be used to frame all 3 dimensions of the cube.*

3a. A row of 100 small cm cubes fit along an edge of the meter cube. An array of 100 x 100 cover the bottom. Finally, 100 of these 100 x 100 layers fill it to the top:

$$100 \times 100 \times 100 = 1{,}000{,}000 \text{ cm cubes} = 1 \text{ million cm}^3$$

3b. Yes. The final term in the sequence of volumes from the previous activity also lists the number of cm³ in 1 m³. This number is 10^6, or 1 million.

4a. A cm cube measures 10 mm x 10 mm x 10 mm, or 1,000 mm³. That is, 1,000 tiny mm cubes fill it completely.

4b. $1 \text{ m}^3 \times \dfrac{10^6 \text{ cm}^3}{1 \text{ m}^3} \times \dfrac{10^3 \text{ mm}^3}{1 \text{ cm}^3} = 10^9 \text{ mm}^3 = 1{,}000{,}000{,}000 \text{ mm}^3 = 1 \text{ billion mm}^3$

Materials
☐ String.
☐ Scissors.
☐ A meter stick.
☐ Metric cubes from the previous activity.
☐ Cellophane tape.

(TO) visualize, with the aid of metric volumes, the number of stars in the Milky Way. To define a personal view of your place in the universe.

OUR SMALL SPECK ◯　　　Metric Measure (　)

1. Sprinkle salt on this mm grid. Examine the grains with a magnifying glass and pin.
    a. What is the overall shape of most salt grains?
    b. If salt grains average 1/2 mm on a side, how many fill a mm³? Draw an enlarged picture to show how they stack together.

EACH SQUARE = 1 mm²

2. Estimate how many grains it would take to fill a cubic meter. Show your work.

3. Our sun is only 1 of at least 200 billion stars in the Milky Way Galaxy.
    a. If each star (including our sun) is represented by a single grain of salt, how many cubic meters represent all the stars in the Milky Way?
    b. Measure out a 5 x 5 meter area in your classroom. How high would the salt reach if it evenly covers this much area?
    c. All these grains represent the stars in just our galaxy. There are perhaps 100 billion galaxies in the universe! What do you make of that?

YOU ARE HERE
MILKY WAY GALAXY

© 1992 by TOPS Learning Systems

Answers / Notes

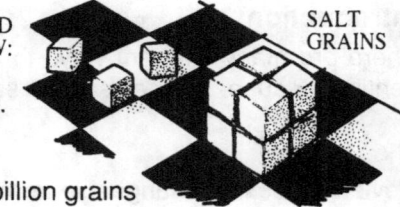
ENLARGED VIEW:　SALT GRAINS

1a. Most of the salt grains are shaped like tiny cubes.

1b. Four average salt grains pushed together seem to cover a black mm square. Four additional grains, stacked neatly on top, would occupy a mm cube.

2. $1\ m^3 \times \dfrac{10^9\ mm^3}{1\ m^3} \times \dfrac{8\ grains}{1\ mm^3} = 8\times 10^9$ grains = 8,000,000,000 grains = 8 billion grains

3a. $200\times 10^9\ stars \times \dfrac{1\ grain}{1\ star} \times \dfrac{1\ m^3\ salt}{8\times 10^9\ grains} = 25\ m^3$ salt

3b. These 25 cubic meters of salt would completely cover a 5 x 5 meter area when stacked side by side. This much salt would thus reach 1 meter high.

3c. *This is a wide open question inviting response or speculation at any level:*

(1) If the Milky Way is an average galaxy, there are:

100×10^9 galaxies $\times \dfrac{200 \times 10^9\ stars}{galaxy} = 20{,}000 \times 10^{18}$ stars $= 2 \times 10^{22}$ stars in the universe.

(2) If each *galaxy* were represented by a salt grain, then the known universe would form a 5 x 5 x .5 meter block of salt grains equal to a volume of 12.5 m³. Moreover, if ours is an average galaxy, then each and every "galaxy" in this pile would further contain enough stars to make its own 25 m³ block of salt grains.

(3) I am a very small piece of the universe.

(4) How wonderful that I, such a small piece of the universe, am able to imagine the whole thing.

(5) The chances of life evolving somewhere else, near some of these salt grain "suns" seems pretty good. But how would we ever find or recognize each other?

(6) If God created life on Earth alone, then life is very special and so are we.

Materials

☐ Table salt.　☐ A straight pin.　☐ Results from the previous activity: 1 billion cubic mm occupy a cubic meter.
☐ A hand lens.　☐ A meter stick.

(TO) calculate the area of a circle, and the volume of a cylinder. To understand volume as area extended through a third dimension.

SIZING UP A CYLINDER   Metric Measure ( )

1. Get a square grid with an inscribed circle. Cut it out neatly on the dashed line.
   a. Count the centimeter squares that occupy just 1 corner. These lay *inside* the square but *outside* the circle.
   b. Use this result to estimate the area of the whole circle. Show your work.
2. The area of a circle is given by $A = \pi r^2$. Check your estimate in step 1 by applying this formula.
3. Rest your grid on the 1 cm cube. What is the total volume of space under the square? Under the circle?
4. Rest your grid on the 3 cm cube. What is the total volume of space under the square? Under the circle?
5. Make a generalization. Tell how to calculate the volume of any area extended into its 3rd dimension.
6. Apply what you've learned. Calculate the volume *inside* a can to the nearest $.1 cm^3$.

(Stick a name tag on your can. Save it and your square grid for later use.)

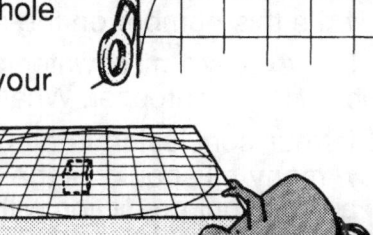

© 1992 by TOPS Learning Systems

Answers / Notes

1a. 5 1/2 squares occupy a corner. *(There are 3 whole squares, plus almost 1/2 more that cover the central area. Another 3 partial squares lie to either side, adding up to about 2 more whole squares.)*

1b. The area of the circle equals the area of the 10 x 10 cm square less the area of its four outside corners:
$$100 \text{ cm}^2 - 4(5.5) \text{ cm}^2 = 78.0 \text{ cm}^2.$$

2. *Remind students, if necessary, that $\pi = 3.14$ or $22/7$; that $r = d/2$.*
$A = \pi r^2 = 3.14 (5)^2 = 78.5 \text{ mm}^2$. This closely agrees with the number of squares counted in step 1.

3. The 100 cm² area of the square, extended 1 cm down, defines a volume of 100 cm³. Similarly the smaller 78.5 cm² area of the circle defines a smaller volume of 78.5 cm³.

4. $V_{\text{under square}} = 100 \text{ cm}^2 (3 \text{ cm}) = 300 \text{ cm}^3.$
    $V_{\text{under circle}} = 78.5 \text{ cm}^2 (3 \text{ cm}) = 235.5 \text{ cm}^3.$

5. The volume of any horizontal surface that extends up or down into the 3rd dimension is area x height, or area x depth.

6. These calculations are based on a 15 ounce vegetable can, with an inside diameter of 7.4 cm and a height of 10.9 cm.
   $r = d/2 = 7.4 \text{ cm}/2 = 3.7 \text{ cm}$
   $A = \pi r^2 = 3.14 (3.7 \text{ cm})^2 = 43.0 \text{ cm}^2.$
   $V_{\text{can}} = A_{\text{top}} \times \text{depth} = 43.0 \text{ cm}^2 \times 10.9 \text{ cm} = 468.7 \text{ cm}^3.$

Materials

☐ A square grid with inscribed circle. Photocopy this from the supplementary page.
☐ Scissors.
☐ The metric cubes constructed in activity 4.
☐ An empty can. Our calculations are based on a 15 ounce vegetable can.
☐ A metric ruler. Photocopy this from the supplementary page.
☐ A calculator (optional).

(TO) discover that dry measure in cm³ is equal to liquid measure in ml. To appreciate the advantages of using each kind of measure.

LIQUID VOLUME ○ Metric Measure (   )

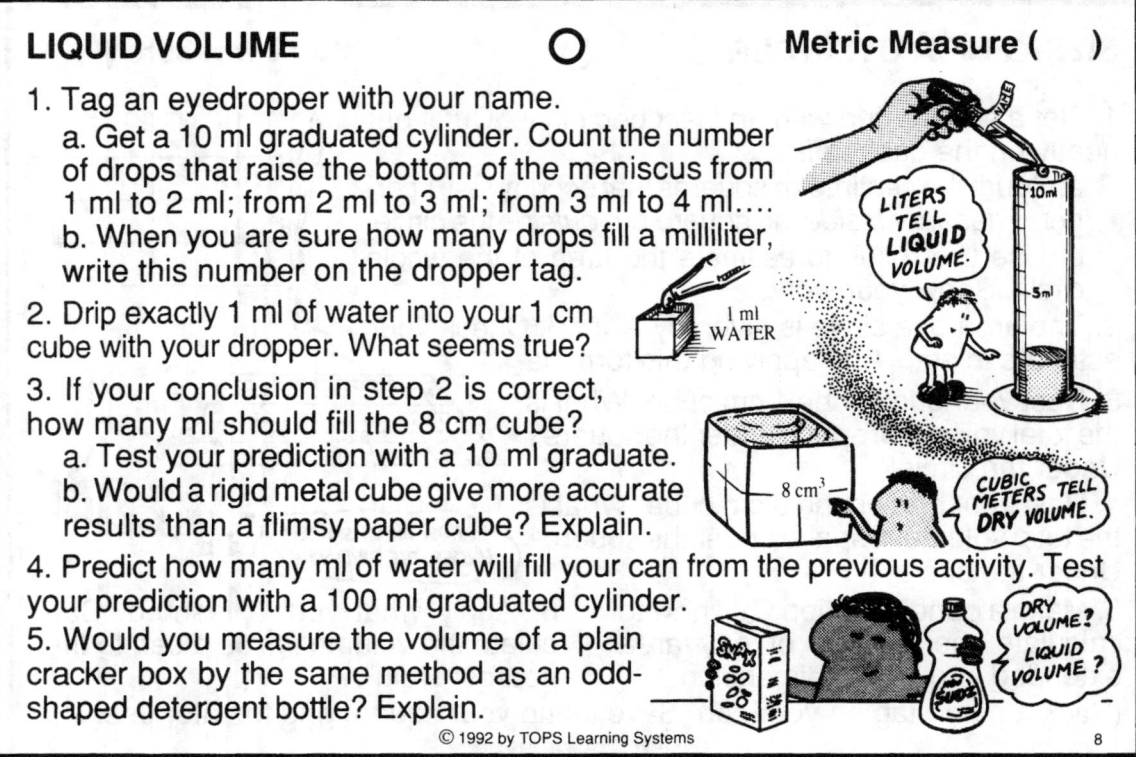

1. Tag an eyedropper with your name.
    a. Get a 10 ml graduated cylinder. Count the number of drops that raise the bottom of the meniscus from 1 ml to 2 ml; from 2 ml to 3 ml; from 3 ml to 4 ml….
    b. When you are sure how many drops fill a milliliter, write this number on the dropper tag.
2. Drip exactly 1 ml of water into your 1 cm cube with your dropper. What seems true?
3. If your conclusion in step 2 is correct, how many ml should fill the 8 cm cube?
    a. Test your prediction with a 10 ml graduate.
    b. Would a rigid metal cube give more accurate results than a flimsy paper cube? Explain.
4. Predict how many ml of water will fill your can from the previous activity. Test your prediction with a 100 ml graduated cylinder.
5. Would you measure the volume of a plain cracker box by the same method as an odd-shaped detergent bottle? Explain.

© 1992 by TOPS Learning Systems

Answers / Notes

1a. Our dropper delivered 18 drops/ml. Other droppers may give different results.

2. One ml of water (in our case 18 drops) fills the 1 cm paper cube to the top. Thus, 1 ml appears to be equivalent to 1 cm³. *(If the cube is set on a dry surface, and the water is free of soap, surface tension will prevent it from leaking out of a reasonably well-constructed paper cube. Once the paper becomes soaked, however, or if it sits in a puddle, the cube will leak easily.)*

3. If 1 ml = 1 cm³, then the 8 cm cube should hold 8 ml.

3a. 8 ml of water fills 8 cm³ almost to the top.

3b. Yes. The paper cube tends to bulge outward when filled with water, creating slightly more volume than 8 cm³. This deformation would not occur with rigid metal sides.

4. In the previous activity this can was calculated to have a volume of 469 cm³. Thus 469 ml of water should fill it level with the top. As predicted, when the can was filled 4 times with a 100 ml graduate, 69 ml more was sufficient to top it off. *(To be absolutely accurate, 1 ml of water equals 1.00027 cm³. This is because each unit of measure is derived from a different standard: a cubic centimeter is dry measure derived from the length of one meter. A milliliter is fluid measure derived from the volume occupied by one gram of water at 4° C.)*

5. No. Use centimeters (dry measure) to find the volume of the cracker box. Measure its length, width and height with a ruler, then multiply these dimensions together. Liquid measure would be inappropriate for a cardboard box that was not water tight.

Use milliliters (liquid measure) to find the volume of the oddly-shaped detergent bottle. Fill it with water from a graduated cylinder, noting the number of ml you add. Dry measure would not be easy to calculate because of its irregular dimensions.

Materials

☐ An eyedropper.
☐ Masking tape.
☐ A 10 ml graduated cylinder.
☐ Water that is free from all traces of soap. Soap breaks the surface tension of water, producing much smaller drops.
☐ The metric cubes constructed in activity 4.
☐ The can from activity 7.
☐ A 100 ml graduated cylinder, or larger.
☐ A pie tin or plate to catch water overflow from the can. Step 4 could also be done in a sink.

(TO) calculate the 1 liter water level in a half-gallon milk carton. To prepare heavy duty buckets to use in the next activity.

LITER BUCKETS ○   Metric Measure (   )

1. Start with 2 half-gallon cardboard milk cartons.
    a. Cut each one to a uniform height of 15 cm.
    b. Paper-punch opposite sides about 2 cm from the rim.
    c. Cut string to 35 cm. Tie handles through the holes.
2. Set one bucket aside. Accurately measure the *inside* length and width of the other. Calculate its *cross-sectional area*.
3. Compare this area to your 10 cm square grid. Which is larger?
    a. How high should you raise your 10 cm square so a 1 liter volume is defined below it?
    b. How high should water in the milk carton reach to define this same 1 liter volume?
    c. Cut a straw equal to this "1 liter height."
4. If you poured 1 liter of water into your bucket (using a 100 ml graduate) should it reach to the top of the straw? Explain.
    a. Test your prediction. (Stick a paper clip into the end of the straw to use as a handle.) Report your findings.
    b. Save both liter-capacity buckets to use again.

© 1992 by TOPS Learning Systems

Answers / Notes

2. A = length x width = (9.5 cm) (9.5 cm) = 90.3 cm².

3. The 10 x 10 cm square grid is larger, with an area of 100 cm².

3a. Raise the square through a distance of 10 cm to define a volume of 1 liter:
    V = area x height = 100 cm² x 10 cm = 1,000 cm³ = 1000 ml = 1 liter.

3b. Because the cross-sectional area of the milk carton is smaller than that of the square grid, it needs to be raised higher to define the same 1 liter volume:

$$\text{height} = \frac{1000 \text{ cm}^3}{90.3 \text{ cm}^2} = 11.1 \text{ cm}$$

4. Yes. One liter of water should reach 11.1 cm up the side of milk carton. This equals the length of the straw.

4a. One liter of water poured from a graduate into the milk carton almost, but not quite, reaches the top of the straw. The carton's liquid capacity is slightly larger than its calculated dry capacity, because its sides bulge out to hold extra water.

Materials

☐ Two half-gallon milk cartons. If your students don't have good scissors, trim these evenly to 15 cm high in advance. Collect and store these finished buckets after activity 15, to use next time you teach this module.
☐ The centimeter ruler photocopied in activity 7.
☐ Scissors.
☐ A paper punch.
☐ String.
☐ A calculator (optional.)
☐ The 10 cm square grid with circle from activity 7.
☐ A source of water. If you don't have a nearby sink, substitute a bucket and dipper cup in all activities that require water.
☐ A straw and paper clip.
☐ A 100 ml graduated cylinder.

(TO) construct a heavy duty equal-arm balance. To make a kilogram standard derived from the mass of one liter of water.

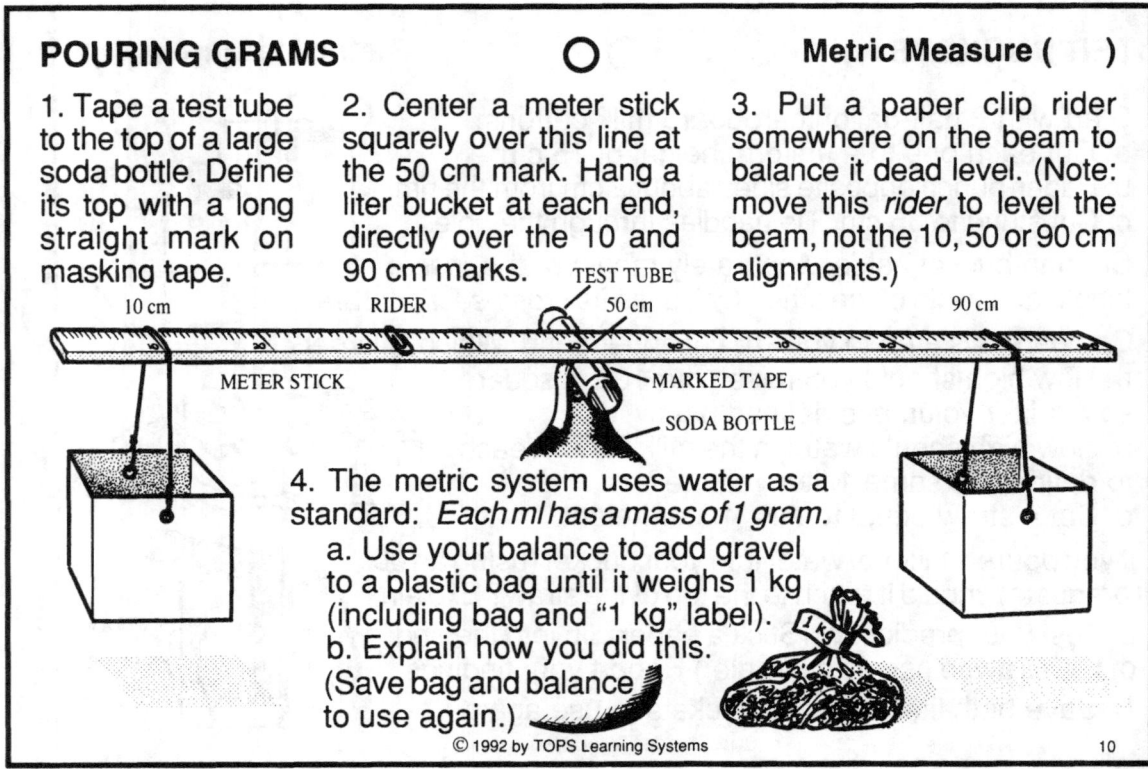

POURING GRAMS   Metric Measure (   )

1. Tape a test tube to the top of a large soda bottle. Define its top with a long straight mark on masking tape.

2. Center a meter stick squarely over this line at the 50 cm mark. Hang a liter bucket at each end, directly over the 10 and 90 cm marks.

3. Put a paper clip rider somewhere on the beam to balance it dead level. (Note: move this *rider* to level the beam, not the 10, 50 or 90 cm alignments.)

4. The metric system uses water as a standard: *Each ml has a mass of 1 gram.*
   a. Use your balance to add gravel to a plastic bag until it weighs 1 kg (including bag and "1 kg" label).
   b. Explain how you did this. (Save bag and balance to use again.)

© 1992 by TOPS Learning Systems

Answers / Notes

3. As the beam tilts right or left, its motion is checked by a small but significant shift of the pivot as it rolls over the test tube in the direction of the tilt. The "uphill" arm thus becomes longer, restoring the beam to a stable horizontal position. If your meter stick is warped upward, raising its center of gravity, a stronger restoring force may be needed. You can substitute a thicker test tube pivot to compensate. Or, if the beam is calibrated in centimeters on both sides, simply turn it over.

4b. First set up the balance as directed at the 10, 50 and 90 cm marks, then position a rider somewhere on the meter stick to make it balance level. Pour exactly one liter of water into one of the buckets. This makes 1 kg:
   1 liter water = 1000 ml = 1000 g = 1 kg.

Line the other bucket with a plastic bag, and stick a tape label marked "1 kg" to the outside. Pour in sand or gravel until it counterbalances the liter of water at the opposite end, then seal the bag with the tape. *(It may be necessary to temporarily lift each bucket off the beam to fill it, then replace it at its proper mark.)*

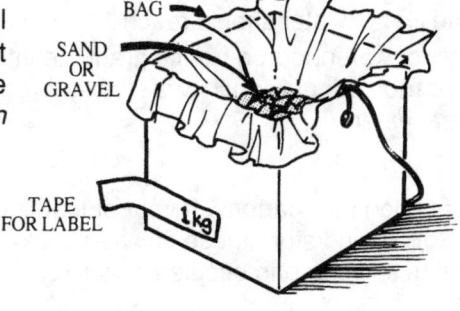

Materials

- A test tube.
- A large soda bottle. Heavy glass bottles are most stable. Lighter plastic 2 liter bottles will also serve. Fill them 1/4 full of water to add ballast.
- Masking tape.
- A meter stick.
- Both liter buckets from activity 9.
- A paper clip. If the liter buckets are cut to equal size, no more than a single paper clip rider should be required to balance the beam. If more weight is required, substitute a heavier washer or lump of clay.
- Water.
- A graduated cylinder, 100 ml or larger.
- A plastic produce bag.
- Gravel or sand.

(TO) explore the properties of a balance beam. To understand that the product of mass and distance must be the same on both sides of a centered beam to achieve balance.

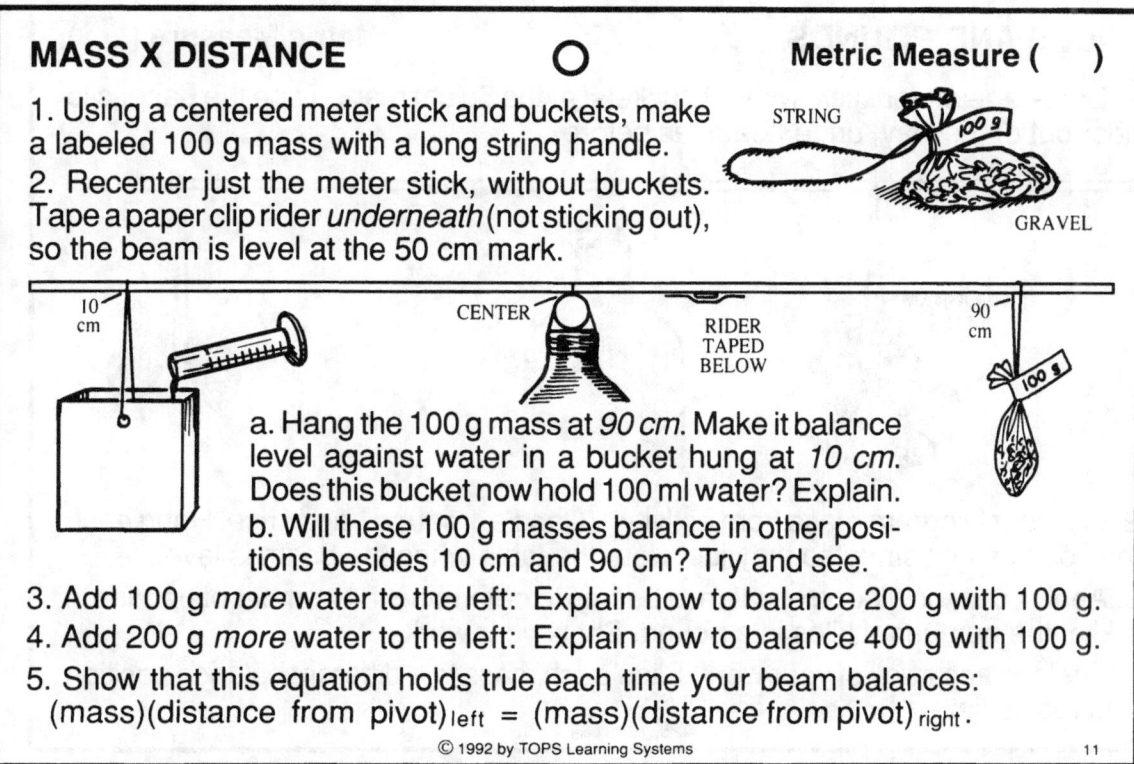

MASS X DISTANCE   Metric Measure ( )

1. Using a centered meter stick and buckets, make a labeled 100 g mass with a long string handle.
2. Recenter just the meter stick, without buckets. Tape a paper clip rider *underneath* (not sticking out), so the beam is level at the 50 cm mark.

   a. Hang the 100 g mass at *90 cm*. Make it balance level against water in a bucket hung at *10 cm*. Does this bucket now hold 100 ml water? Explain.
   b. Will these 100 g masses balance in other positions besides 10 cm and 90 cm? Try and see.
3. Add 100 g *more* water to the left: Explain how to balance 200 g with 100 g.
4. Add 200 g *more* water to the left: Explain how to balance 400 g with 100 g.
5. Show that this equation holds true each time your beam balances:
   (mass)(distance from pivot)$_{left}$ = (mass)(distance from pivot)$_{right}$.

© 1992 by TOPS Learning Systems

Answers / Notes

1. *The gravel, plastic bag, string and tape — everything — should be balanced in one bucket against a 100 ml portion of water in the other bucket.*
   The string loop has optimal length if the bag just clears the table when it is looped over a leveled meter stick.
2. *The top and sides of the meter stick must be kept clear of any paper clip projection to facilitate unrestricted movement of the string handles along the meter stick.*
2a. *No. The water* and *bucket together have a mass of 100 g. Thus the water alone contains less than 100 ml.*
2b. *Yes. Equal masses balance at any position, as long as they are equidistant from the center pivot at 50 cm. Example: 100 g at 20 cm balances 100 g at 80 cm. They are both 30 cm from the pivot.*
3. *The 200 g bucket balances at any position that is half as far from the pivot as the 100 g mass. Example: 200 g at 30 cm balances 100 g at 90 cm. The larger is 20 cm from the pivot, while the smaller is 40 cm away.*
4. *The 400 g bucket balances at any position that is one fourth as far from the pivot as the 100 g mass. Example: 400 g at 40 cm balances 100 g at 90 cm. The larger is 10 cm from the pivot, while the smaller is 40 cm away.*
5.   (mass)(distance from pivot)$_{left}$ = (mass)(distance from pivot)$_{right}$

step 2.	step 3.	step 4.
100 g x 30 cm = 100 g x 30 cm	200 g x 20 cm = 100 g x 40 cm	400 g x 10 cm = 100 g x 40 cm
3000 g-cm = 3000 g-cm	4000 g-cm = 4000 g-cm	4000 g-cm = 4000 g-cm

Materials

- ☐ The meter stick balance with paper clip rider from activity 10.
- ☐ A plastic sandwich bag, or larger.
- ☐ String and scissors.
- ☐ Masking tape.
- ☐ Gravel or sand.
- ☐ Water.
- ☐ An eyedropper.
- ☐ A 100 ml graduated cylinder.

(TO) apply balance beam properties in determining an equivalency between kilograms and pounds.

KILOS AND POUNDS   Metric Measure ( )

1. Center the meter stick, without buckets, at the 50 cm mark. Tape the paper clip rider out of the way, underneath, as before.

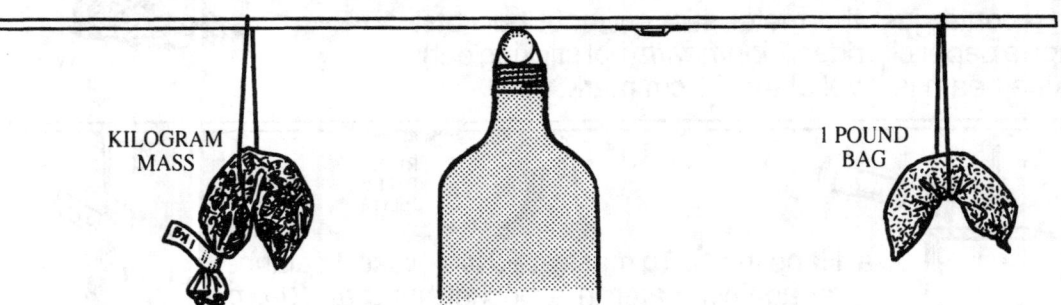

KILOGRAM MASS   1 POUND BAG

2. Get your kilogram mass from activity 10, and a 1 pound bag of rice. Hang each in a loop of light string so they just clear the table when the beam is level.

3. Apply your knowledge of balance beams to determine the number of pounds in a kilo; the number of kilos in a pound. Show your work.

4. Test the accuracy of your work. Slide each mass to a different balance position and recalculate.

© 1992 by TOPS Learning Systems

Answers / Notes

2. *Light kite string is used to support the one kilogram mass and one pound weight. The heavier buckets cannot be substituted, since they would add more than negligible weight to each standard.*

3. In our case, the kilogram standard resting at 31.3 cm balanced the pound standard resting at 90.0 cm:

Distance from pivot:

$$\begin{array}{cc} 50.0 \text{ cm} & 90.0 \text{ cm} \\ -31.3 \text{ cm} & -50.0 \text{ cm} \\ \hline \text{kilo standard} = 18.7 \text{ cm} & \text{pound standard} = 40.0 \text{ cm} \end{array}$$

The beam balances when: (mass)(distance from pivot)$_{left}$ = (mass)(distance from pivot)$_{right}$
(1 kg)(18.7 cm) = (1 lb)(40.0 cm)

Divide to find equivalencies: $1 \text{ kg} = \frac{40.0 \text{ cm}}{18.7 \text{ cm}} \times 1 \text{ lb} = 2.14 \text{ lb}$ $1 \text{ lb} = \frac{18.7 \text{ cm}}{40.0 \text{ cm}} \times 1 \text{ kg} = .47 \text{ kg}$

(accepted value = 2.20 lb)   *(accepted value = .45 kg)*

4. Other balance positions should produce a nearly identical result.

Errors in this experiment tend to derive more from inaccuracies in the standards themselves (the gross weight of the rice is probably slightly more than 1 pound) than from balance beam manipulations.

Discussion

There are about 2.20 lbs/kilogram. Does this hold true on the moon as well? (No. The 1 kilogram mass exerts force [or weight] only as it is accelerated. On the moon 1 kg weighs less than 1 pound; in space, nothing at all.)

Materials

☐ The meter stick balance with paper-clip rider from activity 10. The accessory buckets are not required.
☐ A 1 pound bag of rice. A 1 pound unit of anything will do, as long as it comes in lightweight packaging, such as a plastic bag, so its gross weight is not significantly higher than its net weight. Rice is recommended only because it is used again in activities 15-18.
☐ The 1 kg gravel bag standard from activity 10.
☐ Light string. Kite string is easier to handle than thread, though both will serve.
☐ A calculator (optional).

(TO) construct a light-duty equal arm balance sensitive to 5 milligrams.

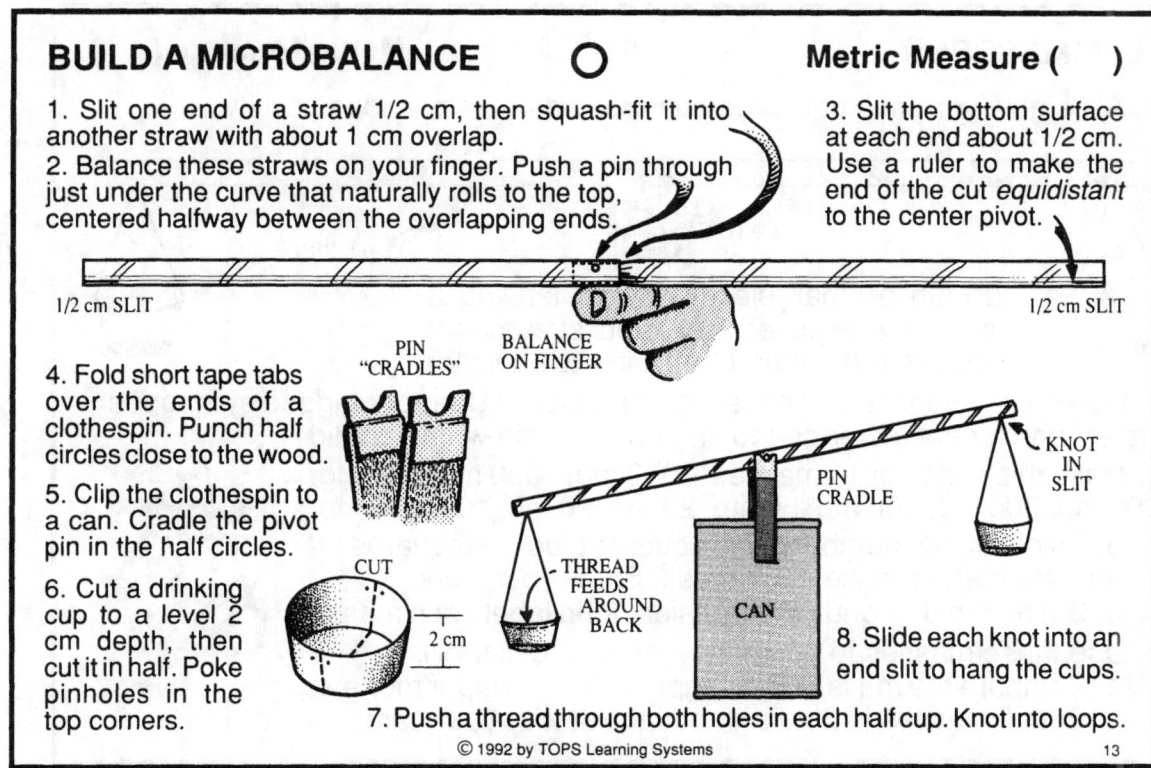

BUILD A MICROBALANCE   Metric Measure (   )

1. Slit one end of a straw 1/2 cm, then squash-fit it into another straw with about 1 cm overlap.

2. Balance these straws on your finger. Push a pin through just under the curve that naturally rolls to the top, centered halfway between the overlapping ends.

3. Slit the bottom surface at each end about 1/2 cm. Use a ruler to make the end of the cut *equidistant* to the center pivot.

4. Fold short tape tabs over the ends of a clothespin. Punch half circles close to the wood.

5. Clip the clothespin to a can. Cradle the pivot pin in the half circles.

6. Cut a drinking cup to a level 2 cm depth, then cut it in half. Poke pinholes in the top corners.

7. Push a thread through both holes in each half cup. Knot into loops.

8. Slide each knot into an end slit to hang the cups.

© 1992 by TOPS Learning Systems

Answers / Notes

1-3. *The overlapping straws, squash-fitted together, will not align perfectly straight. This is OK. The purpose of balancing these straws on the finger is to allow them to roll into their most stable position, thereby establishing a top (for piercing with a pin) and a bottom (for slitting the ends). When the balance pans are hung in step 8, the distance from their point of suspension to central pivot pin should be equal. If this needs adjustment, it is easier to lengthen the end slit of the longer arm, rather than reposition the pivot pin.*

6. *Notice that 1 cup makes two balance pans. This design provides maximum hanging stability with minimum weight.*

8. *The straw beam will not yet balance, not until a rider is added in the next activity.*

Materials

- ☐ Two straws.
- ☐ Scissors.
- ☐ A straight pin.
- ☐ The photocopied metric ruler.
- ☐ Masking tape.
- ☐ A clothespin.
- ☐ A paper punch.
- ☐ A tin can. The can from activity 7 is appropriate.
- ☐ Thread.
- ☐ A paper cup. A styrofoam cup also serves, but will sometimes build up an annoying static charge, clinging to fingers or table top as you try to use the balance.

(TO) develop a series of milligram masses to use with the light-duty balance previously constructed. To accurately determine the mass of a dollar bill and compare paper densities.

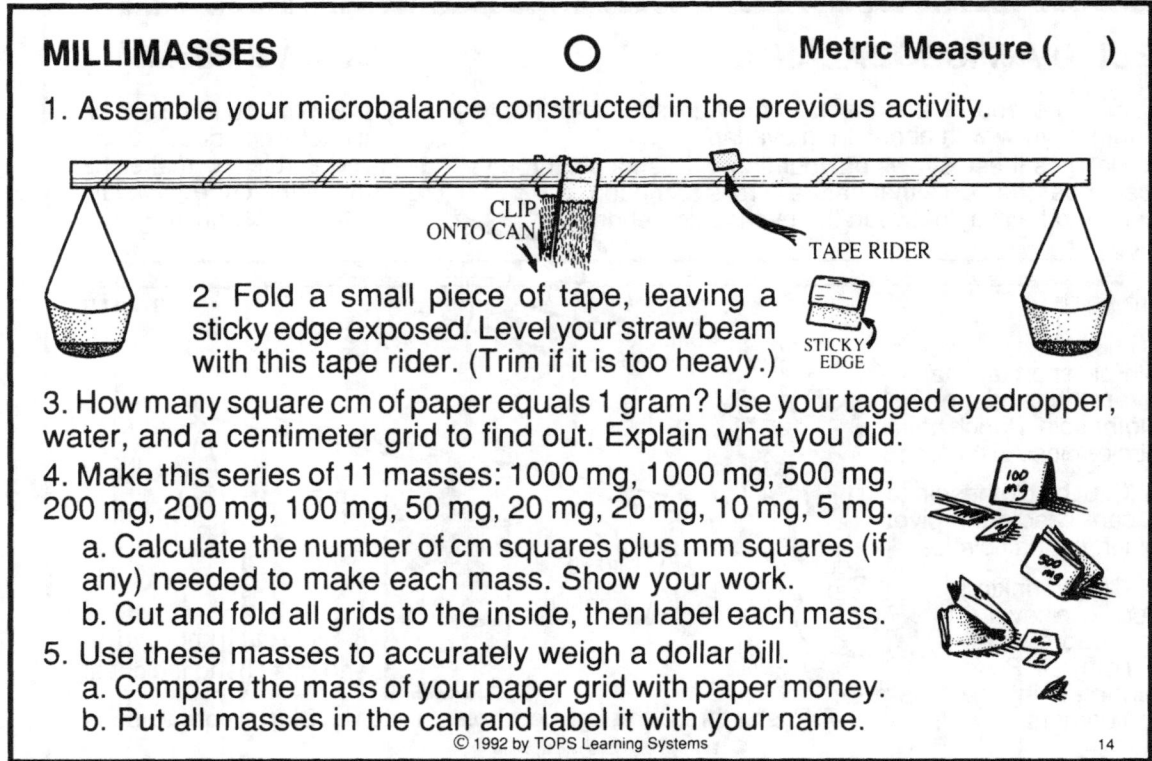

MILLIMASSES ○ Metric Measure ( )

1. Assemble your microbalance constructed in the previous activity.
2. Fold a small piece of tape, leaving a sticky edge exposed. Level your straw beam with this tape rider. (Trim if it is too heavy.)
3. How many square cm of paper equals 1 gram? Use your tagged eyedropper, water, and a centimeter grid to find out. Explain what you did.
4. Make this series of 11 masses: 1000 mg, 1000 mg, 500 mg, 200 mg, 200 mg, 100 mg, 50 mg, 20 mg, 20 mg, 10 mg, 5 mg.
   a. Calculate the number of cm squares plus mm squares (if any) needed to make each mass. Show your work.
   b. Cut and fold all grids to the inside, then label each mass.
5. Use these masses to accurately weigh a dollar bill.
   a. Compare the mass of your paper grid with paper money.
   b. Put all masses in the can and label it with your name.

© 1992 by TOPS Learning Systems

Answers / Notes

3. Drip water into one of the balance pans with the tagged eyedropper, until you measure out 1 gram. Add sections of centimeter grid to the other pan (cut to whole square centimeters), until the straw beam again balances level. Our grid, reproduced on 20 pound copy paper, required 130 cm² to balance.

4a. 1000 mg = 130 cm²
    500 mg = 130 cm² / 2 = 65 cm²
    200 mg = 130 cm² / 5 = 26 cm²
    100 mg = 26 cm² / 2 = 13 cm²
    50 mg = 13 cm² / 2 = 6.5 cm² = 6 cm² + 50 mm²
    20 mg = 26 cm² / 10 = 2.6 cm² = 2 cm² + 60 mm²
    10 mg = 2.6 cm² / 2 = 1.3 cm² = 1 cm² + 30 mm²
    5 mg = 1.3 cm² / 2 = .65 cm² = 65 mm²

5. 1 US dollar = 1 Canadian dollar = 990 ± 20 mg

5a. *To meaningfully compare paper weights, your students must first select equal areas. Since it is cheaper to cut a paper grid to size, the area of a full-sized bill is the reasonable standard of comparison:*

Area of dollar bill = 15.6 cm x 6.6 cm = 103 cm².
Mass of dollar bill = 990 mg.

Area of grid = 103 cm².
Mass of grid = 103 cm² x $\frac{1000 \text{ mg}}{130 \text{ cm}^2}$ = 792 mg.

(This may also be determined without calculation, directly from the microbalance.)

$\frac{\text{mass of dollar}}{\text{mass of grid}} = \frac{990 \text{ mg}}{792 \text{ mg}} = 1.25$

Thus, the dollar is 1.25 times heavier than the paper grid.

Materials

☐ The microbalance constructed in activity 12.
☐ Masking tape.
☐ Scissors.
☐ The tagged eyedropper from activity 8.
☐ Water.
☐ The centimeter grid with millimeter squares. Photocopy this from the supplementary page. Two copies are needed to make all 11 masses unless there are left over grid fragments from earlier activities.
☐ A dollar bill, either US or Canadian.
☐ A calculator (optional).

(TO) find the mass of rice contained in a baby food jar using a balance beam and graduated cylinder.

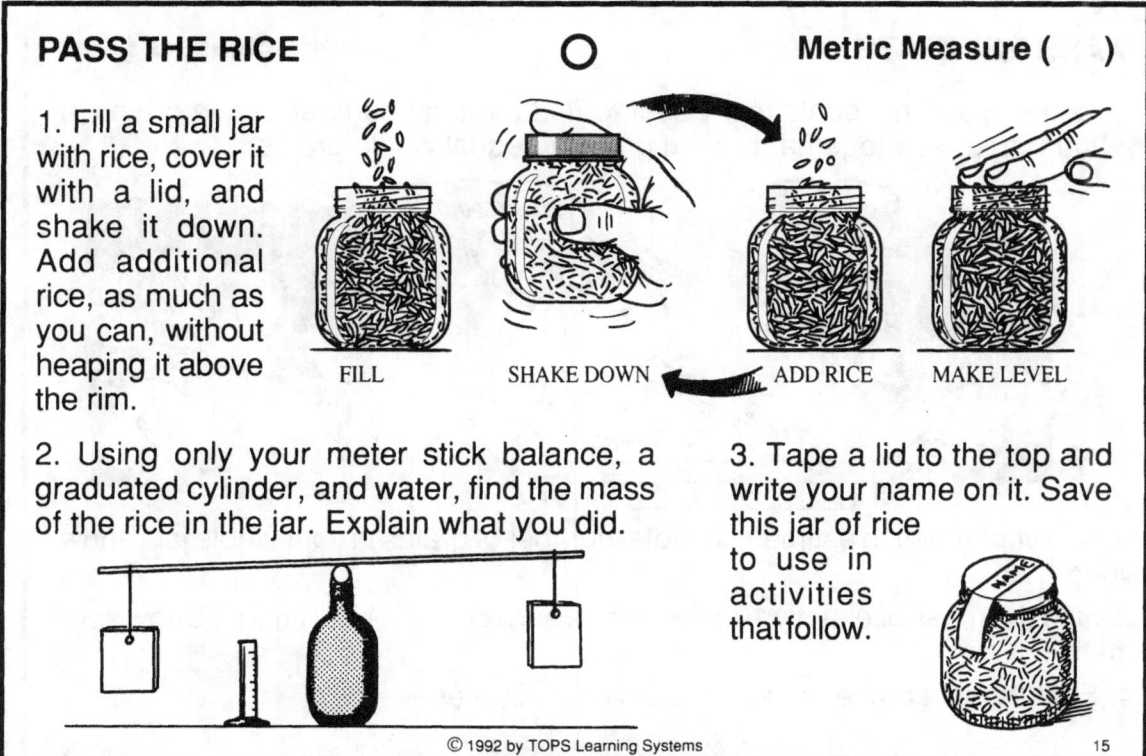

PASS THE RICE — Metric Measure ( )

1. Fill a small jar with rice, cover it with a lid, and shake it down. Add additional rice, as much as you can, without heaping it above the rim.

2. Using only your meter stick balance, a graduated cylinder, and water, find the mass of the rice in the jar. Explain what you did.

3. Tape a lid to the top and write your name on it. Save this jar of rice to use in activities that follow.

© 1992 by TOPS Learning Systems

Answers / Notes

2. Center the meter stick at 50 cm, as before, with *dry* milk-carton buckets equidistant from the pivot at 10 and 90 cm. Then level the beam with a paper clip rider. Pour the jar of rice into one bucket, then add water to the other bucket, bringing the meter stick back into balance. Use the eye dropper, as necessary, to make fine adjustments. Empty *all* the water into a graduated cylinder. The number of ml you collect is the mass of the rice in grams:

$$\text{mass of rice} = 110.0 \text{ ml} = 110.0 \text{ g}$$

The mass of the rice may also be found indirectly by weighing the container with and without the rice inside.

3. *The lid is taped to the jar so it won't be pressed on too tightly and get stuck. If this does occur, twisting it off generally works better than prying it off.*

Materials

☐ A baby food jar with lid. (The calculations here and in later activities are based on 4 oz. capacity jars.)
☐ White rice. (Long-grained rice was used for our sample calculations.)
☐ Masking tape.
☐ The meter stick balance and accessory buckets from activity 10.
☐ A 100 ml graduated cylinder.
☐ Water.
☐ An eyedropper.

(TO) estimate the total number of rice grains in a baby food jar by counting the grains in a small mass and multiplying by the whole.

MASS ESTIMATE **Metric Measure ( )**

1. Center your microbalance. Use it to find the total number of rice grains in 2,000 mg. (Piece together broken grains to equal whole grains).

2. Use your result to estimate the total number of grains in your whole jar. Show your math.
3. Find the mass of exactly 100 rice grains and repeat your estimate. Show your math.
4. Find the difference between your two estimates.

© 1992 by TOPS Learning Systems   16

Answers / Notes

1. Our 2.000 gram sample contained 111 rice grains.

2. The total mass of the rice in the jar was previously determined to be 110.0 grams.

$$\frac{111 \text{ grains}}{2.000 \text{ g}} \times 110.0 \text{ g} = 6{,}105 \text{ grains}$$

3. 100 rice grains has a mass of 1760 mg or 1.760 g.

$$\frac{100 \text{ grains}}{1.760 \text{ g}} \times 110.0 \text{ g} = 6{,}250 \text{ grains}$$

4. Difference between estimates = 6,250 grains – 6,105 grains = 145 grains.

   Consider asking your students to reserve the 100 whole grains from step 3 in a separate dry test tube or 10 ml graduated cylinder, and seal it with a paper plug. The next activity begins with 100 grains of rice which they won't have to recount.

Materials

☐ The microbalance and milligram masses from activities 13-14.
☐ Experimental results from the previous activity, plus the jar of rice.
☐ A calculator (optional).

(TO) estimate the total number of rice grains in a baby food jar by counting the grains in a small volume and multiplying by the whole.

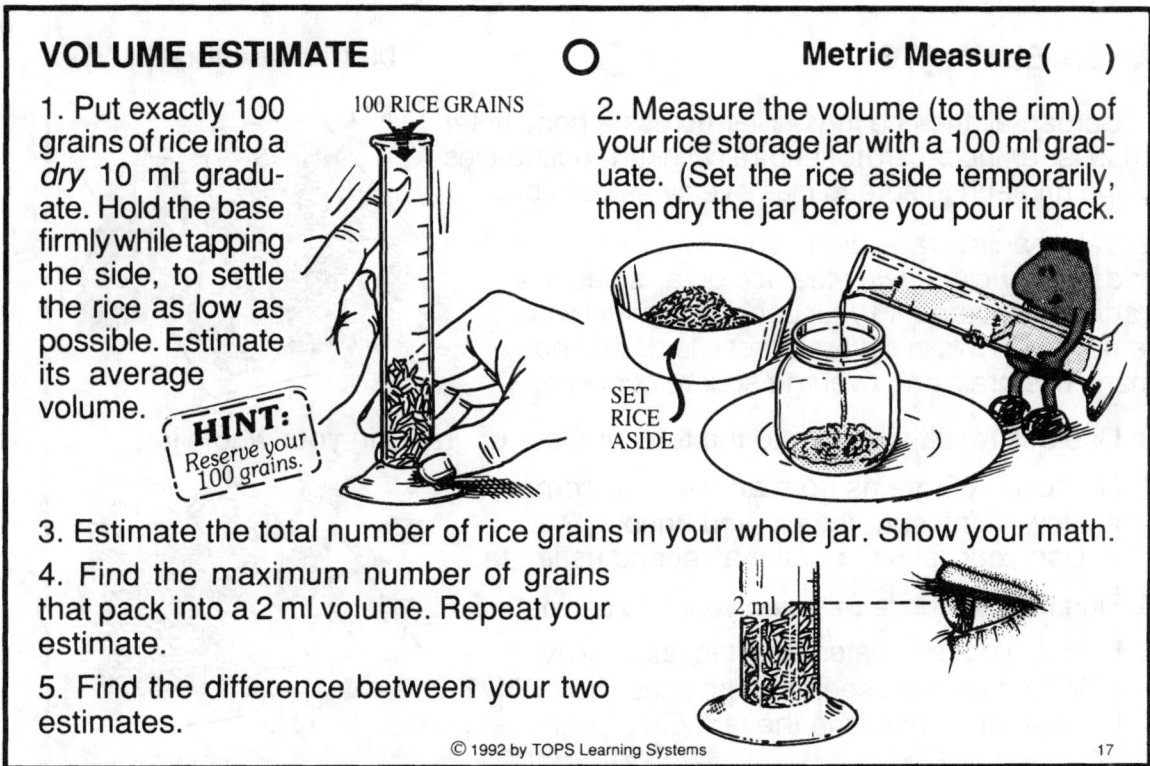

VOLUME ESTIMATE ○   Metric Measure ( )

1. Put exactly 100 grains of rice into a *dry* 10 ml graduate. Hold the base firmly while tapping the side, to settle the rice as low as possible. Estimate its average volume.

HINT: Reserve your 100 grains.

2. Measure the volume (to the rim) of your rice storage jar with a 100 ml graduate. (Set the rice aside temporarily, then dry the jar before you pour it back.)

3. Estimate the total number of rice grains in your whole jar. Show your math.

4. Find the maximum number of grains that pack into a 2 ml volume. Repeat your estimate.

5. Find the difference between your two estimates.

© 1992 by TOPS Learning Systems

Answers / Notes

1. Our 100 grain sample packed down to about 2.2 ml. A few rice grains projected above this graduated mark, but these averaged out with surface gaps extending below the mark.

   (Your students can again avoid counting out rice grains by reserving these 100 grains in the 10 ml graduate to use in step 4.)

2. Adding 127 ml of water to the rice jar brought its water level even with the top. *(It is easier to pour water from the graduate into an empty jar, than from a full jar into the graduate.)*

   While water molecules pack into large or small containers with equal density, rice grains do not. When rice from our 127 ml jar was packed as firmly as possible into the small graduate (10 ml at a time) we found that it occupied 133.6 ml, an increase of 6.6 ml. In activity 18, you might encourage your class to undertake a similar investigation as they evaluate which estimating method they think is most accurate.

3. $\frac{100 \text{ grains}}{2.2 \text{ ml}} \times 127 \text{ ml} = 5773$ grains

4. A maximum of 92 rice grains seem to pack down into a 2.0 ml volume. It was necessary to remove about 8 of the 100 grains to achieve this volume.

   $\frac{92 \text{ grains}}{2.0 \text{ ml}} \times 127 \text{ ml} = 5842$ grains

5. Difference between estimates = 5842 grains − 5773 grains = 109 grains.

Materials

☐ A 10 ml graduate. (This will contain 100 rice grains if they were saved as recommended in the last activity.)
☐ The jar of rice from activity 15.
☐ A 100 ml graduate and water.
☐ A paper towel.
☐ A pie plate or other overflow container may be useful, unless the rice jar is filled over a sink.
☐ A dry container to temporarily store rice from the jar.
☐ A calculator (optional).

(TO) estimate the total number of rice grains in a baby food jar by spreading all the rice over a centimeter grid, then counting the average number of grains in a typical square.

AREA ESTIMATE   ○   Metric Measure ( )

1. Spread all the rice in your jar across a centimeter grid. Use an index card to keep it all within the boundaries of the grid and to spread it as evenly as possible.

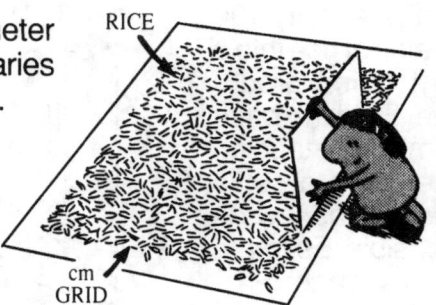

2. Select an average depth somewhere on your grid. Gently clear away the rice on all sides of a particular square with your pencil and count what remains. Do this in several places to decide how many rice grains an average square contains.

3. Use this result to estimate the total number of grains in your whole jar.

4. Remove 100 grains from an average corner.
   a. How many squares did you uncover?
   b. Use your result to make a second estimate.

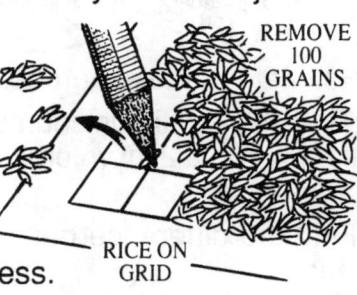

5. Find the difference between your two estimates.

6. Review your estimates over the last 3 activities.
   a. Which method seems most accurate? Why?
   b. How much rice is in the jar? Give your best guess.

© 1992 by TOPS Learning Systems

Answers / Notes

2. On average, there are about 14 rice grains per cm^2.

3. Total area of grid = 18 cm x 25 cm = 450 cm^2.

$$\frac{14 \text{ grains}}{cm^2} \times 450 \text{ cm}^2 = 6,300 \text{ grains}$$

4a. Removing 100 rice grains exposed about 8 squares

4b. $\frac{100 \text{ grains}}{8 \text{ cm}^2} \times 450 \text{ cm}^2 = 5,625 \text{ grains}$

5. Difference between estimates:
   6,300 grains − 5,624 grains = 675 grains.

6a. The area estimate is least accurate since it is difficult to spread all rice grains over the paper to a uniform depth, and hard to isolate the grains contained in any one square. The volume and mass estimates both fall within a narrower range, yet differ significantly. We found that rice packs less densely in a narrow 10 ml graduate than in its wider storage jar, causing the volume estimates to fall too low.

6b. Assuming the mass estimates to be most accurate, our best guess is a range of values consistent with activity 16: about 6,180 ± 100 rice grains.

Discussion

Draw a frequency chart on your blackboard. Record the distribution of all the estimates in your class using these codes: m = mass, v = volume, a = area. In your discussion, encourage students to speculate why volume estimates are consistently less than mass estimates; why area estimates are probably the most widely distributed. Encourage scientific debate. Try to settle disagreements by experiment.

If one of the jars is emptied, and the rice grains are distributed, say 5 ml per student to a class of 25, then all the grains can be counted in just a few minutes. Your class may need to negotiate whose jar gets to be counted.

Materials

☐ The jar of rice from activity 15.
☐ A centimeter grid. Photocopy this from the supplementary page.
☐ An index card. A pencil will also serve.
☐ A calculator (optional).

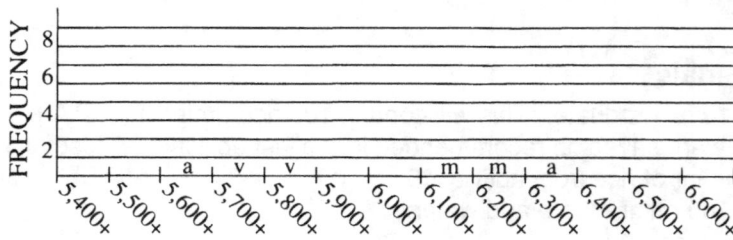

(TO) explain an apparent area gain in a group of puzzle pieces.

HOW CAN THIS BE?   Metric Measure ( )

1. Draw *two* triangles and *two* trapezoids on a centimeter grid like these. Cut them out.

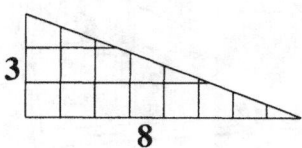 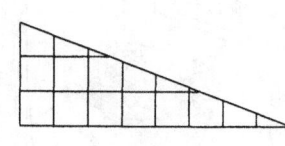 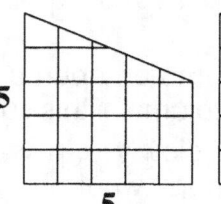 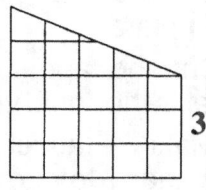

2. Put the four pieces together to form an 8 x 8 cm square.
   a. Sketch your solution.
   b. What is the area of this square?

3. Rearrange the four pieces to form a 5 x 13 cm rectangle.
   a. Sketch your solution.
   b. What is the area of this rectangle?

4. Identical puzzle pieces assemble into two shapes with different areas! How can this be?

© 1992 by TOPS Learning Systems

Answers / Notes

2. area = 8 cm x 8 cm = 64 cm².

3. area = 5 cm x 13 cm = 65 cm².

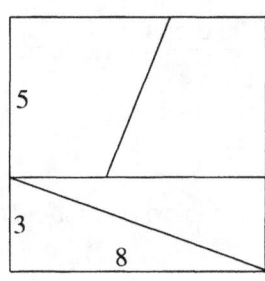 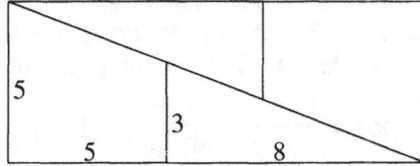

4. There is a 1 cm² open gap in the center of the 65 cm² rectangle. It contains 64 cm² of paper plus 1 cm² of space. *(This gap is easiest to detect if students redraw triangles and trapezoids on an uncut centimeter grid, as they fit together inside the 5 x 13 rectangle.)*

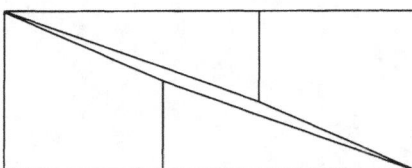

Materials
☐ A centimeter grid. Use the grid left over from the previous activity.
☐ Scissors.
☐ An index card to serve as a straight edge.

notes 19   enrichment

(TO) use the metric system to estimate how long it takes a dripping faucet to waste a metric ton of water.

A TON OF WATER   Metric Measure ( )

1. Draw a 10 cm cube pattern on newspaper. Use your 10 cm square as a template.

2. Cut and tape it into an open cube. What is the liquid volume of this cube?

3. Make a faucet slowly drip water. How many total drops would fill your model (if it didn't leak)?

4. Assume your faucet drips one drop per second. How long would it take to fill your cube?

5. How long would it take your dripping faucet to fill a whole cubic meter?

6. A metric ton equals 1,000 kg. If you failed to fix your dripping faucet, how much time would pass before you wasted a ton of water?

...OUGHT TO FIX THAT ONE OF THESE DAYS...

DRIP
DRIP
DRIP

© 1992 by TOPS Learning Systems

Answers / Notes

2. The liquid volume equals 1 liter, or 1,000 ml.

3. *Since the newspaper cube doesn't hold water, students should collect and measure the drops in something that does. We found that 25 drops from our faucet filled a 10 ml graduate to its top calibration:*

$$\frac{25 \text{ drops}}{10 \text{ ml}} \times 1{,}000 \text{ ml} = 2{,}500 \text{ drops}$$

4. $2{,}500 \text{ drops} \times \frac{1 \text{ sec}}{1 \text{ drop}} \times \frac{1 \text{ min}}{60 \text{ sec}} = 41.7$ minutes

5. There are 1,000 liters in a cubic meter. *(This can be confirmed using the cubic meter model from activity 5.)*

$$1 \text{ m}^3 \times \frac{1{,}000 \text{ liters}}{1 \text{ m}^3} \times \frac{41.7 \text{ min}}{1 \text{ liter}} \times \frac{1 \text{ hr}}{60 \text{ min}} \times \frac{1 \text{ day}}{24 \text{ hr}} = 29.0 \text{ days}$$

6. One metric ton water = 1,000 kg water = 1,000 liters water = 1 m³ water. Thus, a ton of water is wasted each 29.0 days.

Materials

☐ The 10 cm square grid from activity 7.
☐ Scissors.
☐ A sheet of newspaper.
☐ Cellophane tape or masking tape.
☐ A faucet.
☐ A 10 ml graduate.
☐ A calculator (optional).

REPRODUCIBLE STUDENT TASK CARDS

These Reproducible Student Task Cards may be duplicated for use with this module only, provided such reproductions bear copyright notice. Beyond single-classroom use, reproduction of these task cards by schools or school systems for wider dissemination, or by anyone for commercial sale, is strictly prohibited.

Task Cards Options

Here are 3 management options to consider before you photocopy:

1. Consumable Worksheets: Copy 1 complete set of task card pages. Cut out each card and fix it to a separate sheet of boldly lined paper. Duplicate a class set of each worksheet master you have made, 1 per student. Direct students to follow the task card instructions at the top of each page, then respond to questions in the lined space underneath.

2. Nonconsumable Reference Booklets: Copy and collate the 2-up task card pages in sequence. Make perhaps half as many sets as the students who will use them. Staple each set in the upper left corner, both front and back to prevent the outside pages from working loose. Tell students that these task card booklets are for reference only. They should use them as they would any textbook, responding to questions on their own papers, returning them unmarked and in good shape at the end of the module.

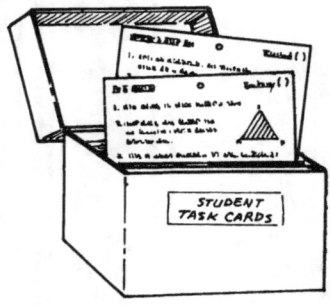

3. Nonconsumable Task Cards: Copy several sets of task card pages. Laminate them, if you wish, for extra durability, then cut out each card to display in your room. You might pin cards to bulletin boards; or punch out the holes and hang them from wall hooks (you can fashion hooks from paper clips and tape these to the wall); or fix cards to cereal boxes with paper fasteners, 4 to a box; or keep cards on designated reference tables. The important thing is to provide enough task card reference points about your classroom to avoid a jam of too many students at any one location. Two or 3 task card sets should accommodate everyone, since different students will use different cards at different times.

DECIMAL LADDER (1)   Metric Measuring (   )

1. Write this equation on the middle line of a sheet of notebook paper, to the right of the margin line: **one = 10^0 = 1**.
2. Follow this pattern *upward*, writing equations 1 line at a time, until you reach a billion.
3. Start again at "one" and go *down* until you reach a billionth.

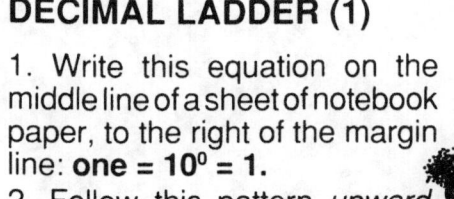

1. ↑
thousand = 10^3 =
hundred = 10^2 = (10)(10) = 100
ten = 10^1 = (10) = 10
one = 10^0 = 1
tenth = 10^{-1} = $1/10^1$ = .1
hundredth = 10^{-2} = $1/10^2$ = .01
2. ↓

4. Think of the lines on notebook paper as rungs on a ladder.

   a. These equations are *one* rung apart. Balance them:
      (?) ten = hundred
      (?) thousand = hundred
      (?) hundredth = tenth
      (?) one = tenth

   b. These equations are *three* rungs apart. Balance them:
      (?) ten = ten thousand
      (?) hundredth = ten
      (?) one = thousandth
      (?) thousandth = millionth

c. How do you balance equations between larger and smaller numbers on this decimal ladder? Invent a rule.

© 1992 by TOPS Learning Systems

DECIMAL LADDER (2)   Metric Measuring (   )

1. Write these metric prefixes to the *left* of the margin, each in its proper place:

kilo / thousand =
hecto / hundred = 10^2
deka / ten = 10^1 = (10) = 10
one = 10^0 = 1
deci / tenth = 10^{-1} = 1/10 = .1
centi / hundredth = 10^{-2} = 1/100 =
milli / thousandth = 10^{-3} =

2. Include these additional prefixes higher and lower on your ladder:

  giga = billion,
  mega = million;
  micro = millionth;
  nano = billionth.

3. Write the *number* equivalent of a: kiloelephant, millipickle, dekarabbit, decidollar, centidollar, megafish, gigastar, nanopart, hectostudent, micropie.

4. Write the *metric* equivalent of: 100 seconds; .1 bushels; a million volts; .001 ounce; 10^{-6} second; 10 inches; 10^9 watts; .01 miles; a billionth gram; 1,000 years.

5. Use your decimal ladder to solve each problem. Explain your reasoning.
   a. Have you ever run a million millimeters? How far is it?
   b. Would you rather have a gigacent or a megadollar?
   c. Can you hold your breath for a kilosecond?
   d. Have you ever slept a milliyear without waking up?

© 1992 by TOPS Learning Systems

DECIMAL LADDER (3) Metric Measuring ( )

1. Write 2 balanced equations for each set of measures. The first one is worked as an example.

   a. centimeters (cm) / millimeters (mm)
   b. kilometers (km) / meters (m)
   c. meters / millimeters (mm)
   d. kilograms (kg) / grams (g)
   e. grams / milligrams (mg)
   f. liters (l) / milliliters (ml)
   g. seconds (s) / microseconds (mcs)
   h. seconds / nanoseconds (ns)
   i. megabytes (mgb) / bytes (b)
   j. gigabytes (gb) / bytes

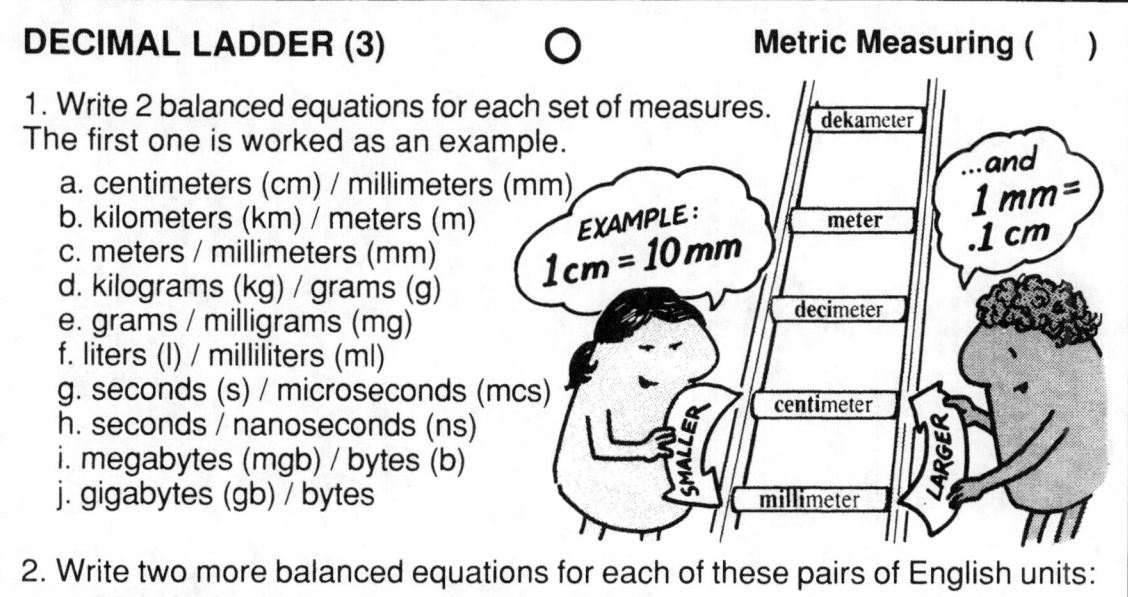

EXAMPLE: 1 cm = 10 mm ...and 1 mm = .1 cm

2. Write two more balanced equations for each of these pairs of English units:
   a. feet / inches   b. pounds / ounces

3. Units are interchangeable in both the metric system and English system. Which system is easier to use? Why?

© 1992 by TOPS Learning Systems

LENGTH, AREA, VOLUME... Metric Measuring ( )

1. Draw 4 "cross" patterns on a centimeter grid. Cut, fold and tape them into a row of cubes of these increasing sizes:

2. Each cube has a unique...
   length: side (s)
   area: surface (s)(s)
   volume: space (s)(s)(s).

SIDE (s) = 1 cm, 2 cm, 3 cm, 4 cm.

List these in three columns, as a sequence of numbers *and* units.

3. Extend the sequence in each column until you reach a cube that measures 10 cm on a side.

4. What is the length, area and volume of a cube measuring 100 cm (1 meter) on a side?

5. What *dimension* does each of these units measure: feet^2, yards^3, m, cm^3, inches, sq km, cubic feet, yards^2, miles, cm^4?

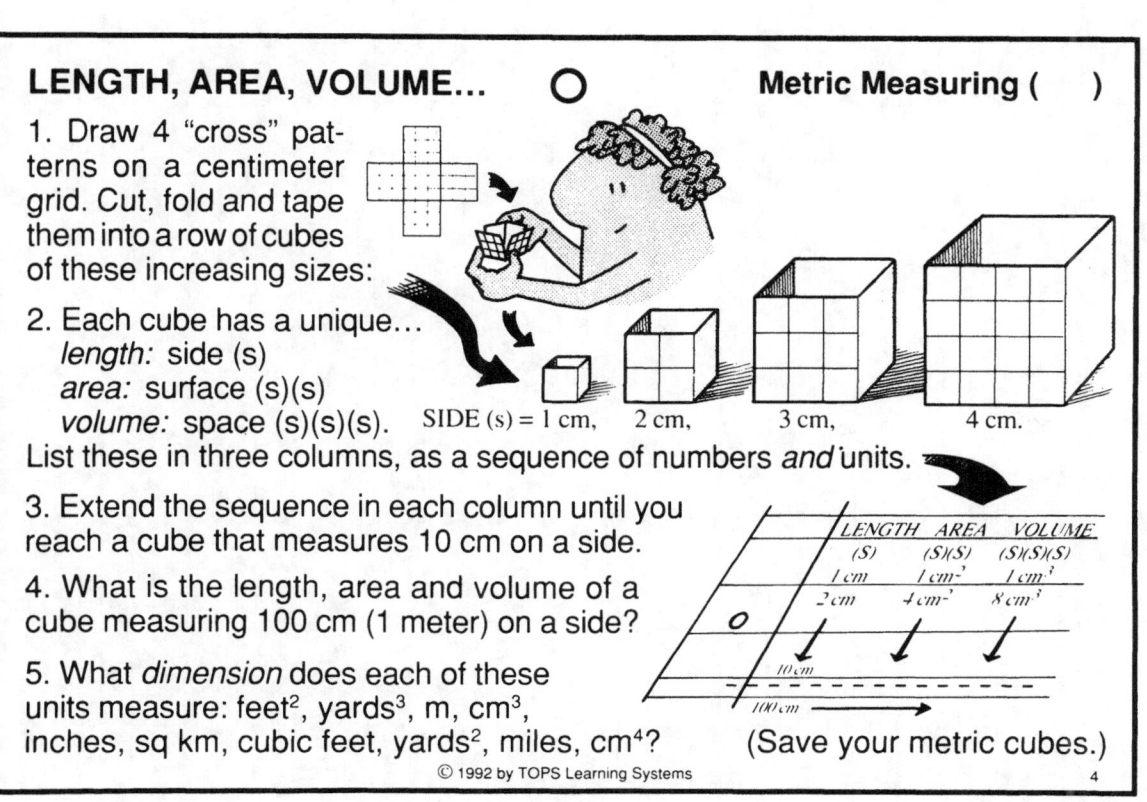

| LENGTH | AREA | VOLUME |
(S)	(S)(S)	(S)(S)(S)
1 cm	1 cm^2	1 cm^3
2 cm	4 cm^2	8 cm^3
10 cm		
100 cm		

(Save your metric cubes.)

© 1992 by TOPS Learning Systems

MILLIONS AND BILLIONS ○ Metric Measuring (   )

1. Cut 3 pieces of string that each measure one meter.

2. Tape them to your largest (4 cm^3) cube, so each string extends outward in a different dimension from the same corner.

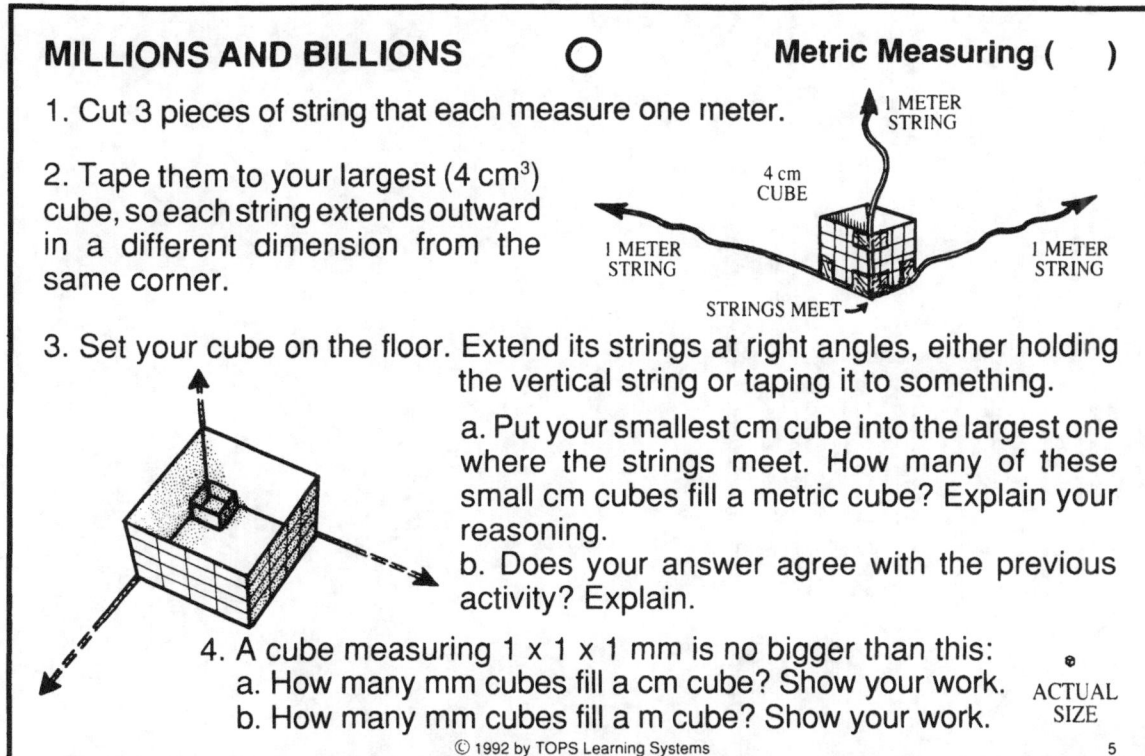

3. Set your cube on the floor. Extend its strings at right angles, either holding the vertical string or taping it to something.

   a. Put your smallest cm cube into the largest one where the strings meet. How many of these small cm cubes fill a metric cube? Explain your reasoning.

   b. Does your answer agree with the previous activity? Explain.

4. A cube measuring 1 x 1 x 1 mm is no bigger than this: • ACTUAL SIZE
   a. How many mm cubes fill a cm cube? Show your work.
   b. How many mm cubes fill a m cube? Show your work.

© 1992 by TOPS Learning Systems

OUR SMALL SPECK ○ Metric Measuring (   )

1. Sprinkle salt on this mm grid. Examine the grains with a magnifying glass and pin.

   a. What is the overall shape of most salt grains?

   b. If salt grains average 1/2 mm on a side, how many fill a mm^3? Draw an enlarged picture to show how they stack together.

EACH SQUARE = 1 mm^2

2. Estimate how many grains it would take to fill a cubic meter. Show your work.

3. Our sun is only 1 of at least 200 billion stars in the Milky Way Galaxy.

   a. If each star (including our sun) is represented by a single grain of salt, how many cubic meters represent all the stars in the Milky Way?

   b. Measure out a 5 x 5 meter area in your classroom. How high would the salt reach if it evenly covers this much area?

   c. All these grains represent the stars in just our galaxy. There are perhaps 100 billion galaxies in the universe! What do you make of that?

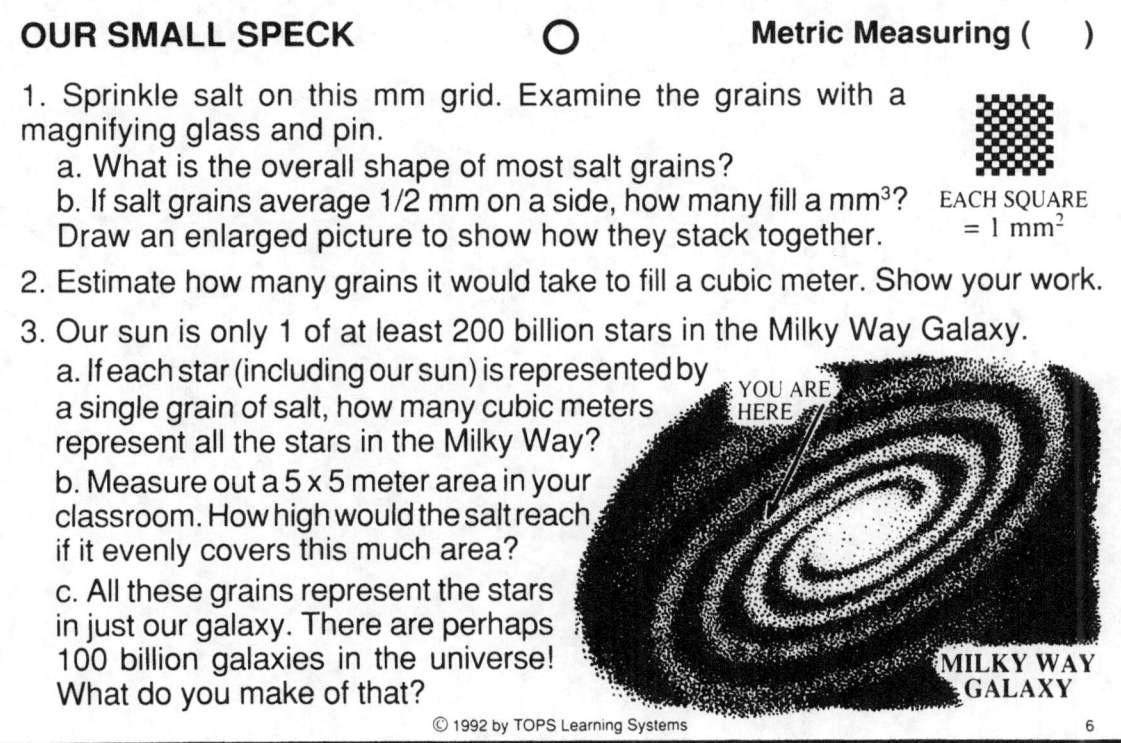

MILKY WAY GALAXY

© 1992 by TOPS Learning Systems

SIZING UP A CYLINDER — Metric Measuring ( )

1. Get a square grid with an inscribed circle. Cut it out neatly on the dashed line.
   a. Count the centimeter squares that occupy just 1 corner. These lay *inside* the square but *outside* the circle.
   b. Use this result to estimate the area of the whole circle. Show your work.
2. The area of a circle is given by $A = \pi r^2$. Check your estimate in step 1 by applying this formula.
3. Rest your grid on the 1 cm cube. What is the total volume of space under the square? Under the circle?
4. Rest your grid on the 3 cm cube. What is the total volume of space under the square? Under the circle?
5. Make a generalization. Tell how to calculate the volume of any area extended into its 3rd dimension.
6. Apply what you've learned. Calculate the volume *inside* a can to the nearest $.1 cm^3$.

(Stick a name tag on your can. Save it and your square grid for later use.)

© 1992 by TOPS Learning Systems   7

LIQUID VOLUME — Metric Measuring ( )

1. Tag an eyedropper with your name.
   a. Get a 10 ml graduated cylinder. Count the number of drops that raise the bottom of the meniscus from 1 ml to 2 ml; from 2 ml to 3 ml; from 3 ml to 4 ml....
   b. When you are sure how many drops fill a milliliter, write this number on the dropper tag.
2. Drip exactly 1 ml of water into your one centimeter paper cube. What seems true?
3. If your conclusion in step 2 is correct, how many ml should fill the 8 cm cube?
   a. Test your prediction with a 10 ml graduate.
   b. Would a rigid metal cube give more accurate results than a flimsy paper cube? Explain.
4. Predict how many ml of water will fill your can from the previous activity. Test your prediction with a 100 ml graduated cylinder.
5. Would you measure the volume of a plain cracker box by the same method as an odd-shaped detergent bottle? Explain.

© 1992 by TOPS Learning Systems   8

LITER BUCKETS   Metric Measuring (   )

1. Start with 2 half-gallon cardboard milk cartons.
   a. Cut each one to a uniform height of 15 cm.
   b. Paper-punch opposite sides about 2 cm from the rim.
   c. Cut string to 35 cm. Tie handles through the holes.
2. Set one bucket aside. Accurately measure the *inside* length and width of the other. Calculate its *cross-sectional area*.
3. Compare this area to your 10 cm square grid. Which is larger?
   a. How high should you raise your 10 cm square so a 1 liter volume is defined below it?
   b. How high should water in the milk carton reach to define this same 1 liter volume?
   c. Cut a straw equal to this "1 liter height."
4. If you poured 1 liter of water into your bucket (using a 100 ml graduate) should it reach to the top of the straw? Explain.
   a. Test your prediction. (Stick a paper clip into the end of the straw to use as a handle.) Report your findings.
   b. Save both liter-capacity buckets to use again.

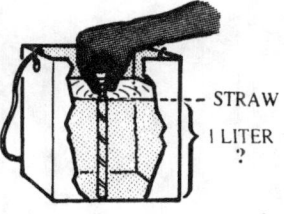

© 1992 by TOPS Learning Systems

POURING GRAMS   Metric Measuring (   )

1. Tape a test tube to the top of a large soda bottle. Define its top with a long straight mark on masking tape.
2. Center a meter stick squarely over this line at the 50 cm mark. Hang a liter bucket at each end, directly over the 10 and 90 cm marks.
3. Put a paper clip rider somewhere on the beam to balance it dead level. (Note: move this *rider* to level the beam, not the 10, 50 or 90 cm alignments.)

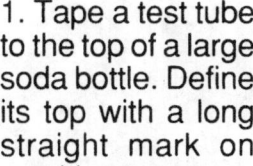
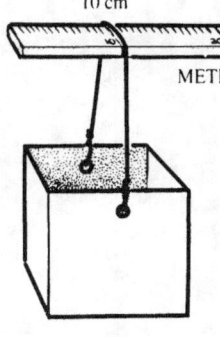
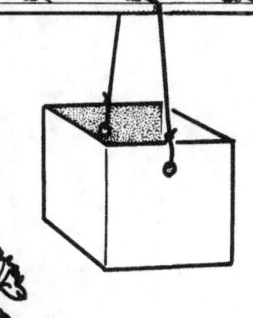

4. The metric system uses water as a standard: *Each ml has a mass of 1 gram.*
   a. Use your balance to add gravel to a plastic bag until it weighs 1 kg (including bag and "1 kg" label).
   b. Explain how you did this. (Save bag and balance to use again.)

© 1992 by TOPS Learning Systems

cards 9-10

MASS X DISTANCE ◯ Metric Measuring ( )

1. Using a centered meter stick and buckets, make a labeled 100 g mass with a long string handle.

2. Recenter just the meter stick, without buckets. Tape a paper clip rider *underneath* (not sticking out), so the beam is level at the 50 cm mark.

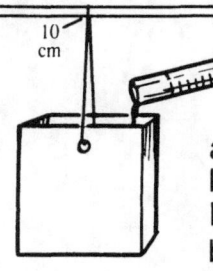

a. Hang the 100 g mass at *90 cm*. Make it balance level against water in a bucket hung at *10 cm*. Does this bucket now hold 100 ml water? Explain.

b. Will these 100 g masses balance in other positions besides 10 cm and 90 cm? Try and see.

3. Add 100 g *more* water to the left: Explain how to balance 200 g with 100 g.

4. Add 200 g *more* water to the left: Explain how to balance 400 g with 100 g.

5. Show that this equation holds true each time your beam balances:
(mass)(distance from pivot)$_{left}$ = (mass)(distance from pivot)$_{right}$.

© 1992 by TOPS Learning Systems

KILOS AND POUNDS ◯ Metric Measuring ( )

1. Center the meter stick, without buckets, at the 50 cm mark. Tape the paper clip rider out of the way, underneath, as before.

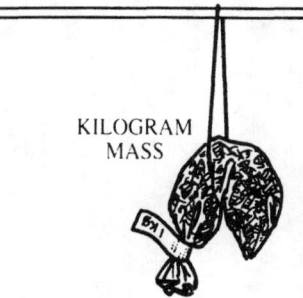

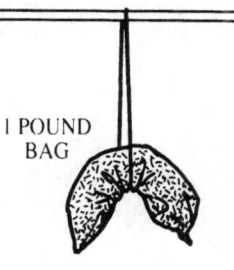

2. Get your kilogram mass from activity 10, and a 1 pound bag of rice. Hang each in a loop of light string so they just clear the table when the beam is level.

3. Apply your knowledge of balance beams to determine the number of pounds in a kilo; the number of kilos in a pound. Show your work.

4. Test the accuracy of your work. Slide each mass to a different balance position and recalculate.

© 1992 by TOPS Learning Systems

BUILD A MICROBALANCE   ◯   Metric Measuring (   )

1. Slit one end of a straw 1/2 cm, then squash-fit it into another straw with about 1 cm overlap.
2. Balance these straws on your finger. Push a pin through just under the curve that naturally rolls to the top, centered halfway between the overlapping ends.
3. Slit the bottom surface at each end about 1/2 cm. Use a ruler to make the end of the cut *equidistant* to the center pivot.

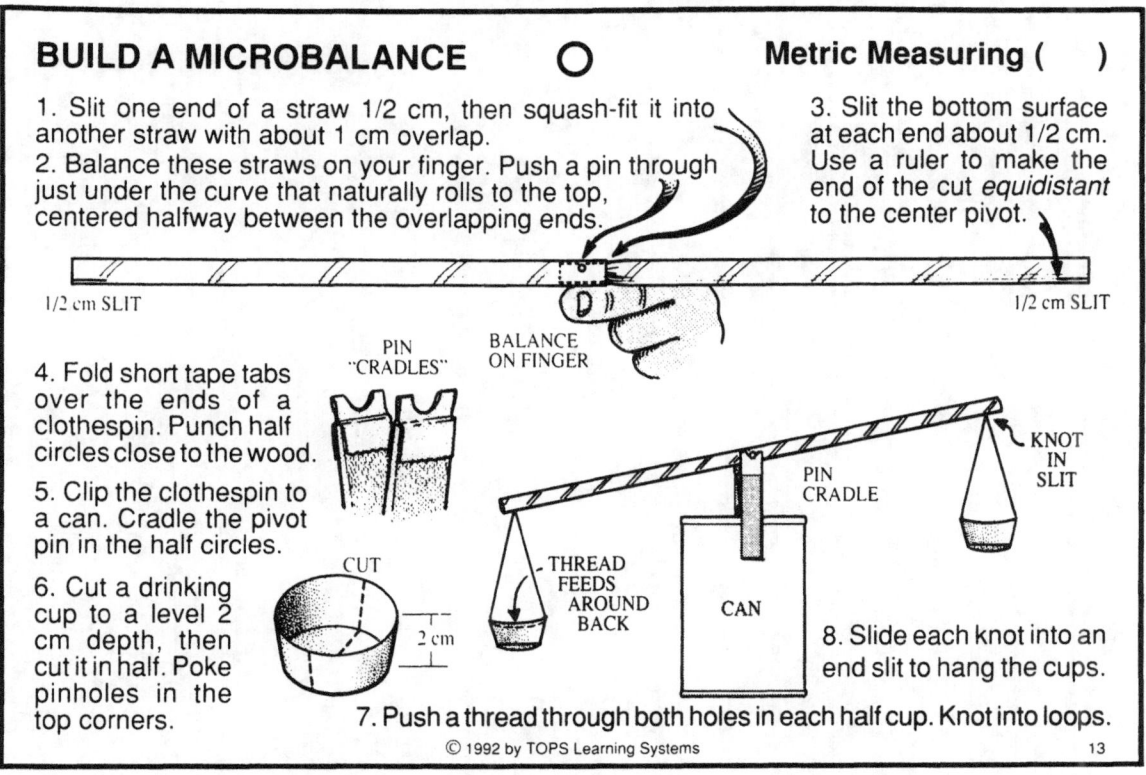

4. Fold short tape tabs over the ends of a clothespin. Punch half circles close to the wood.
5. Clip the clothespin to a can. Cradle the pivot pin in the half circles.
6. Cut a drinking cup to a level 2 cm depth, then cut it in half. Poke pinholes in the top corners.
7. Push a thread through both holes in each half cup. Knot into loops.
8. Slide each knot into an end slit to hang the cups.

© 1992 by TOPS Learning Systems

MILLIMASSES   ◯   Metric Measuring (   )

1. Assemble your microbalance constructed in the previous activity.

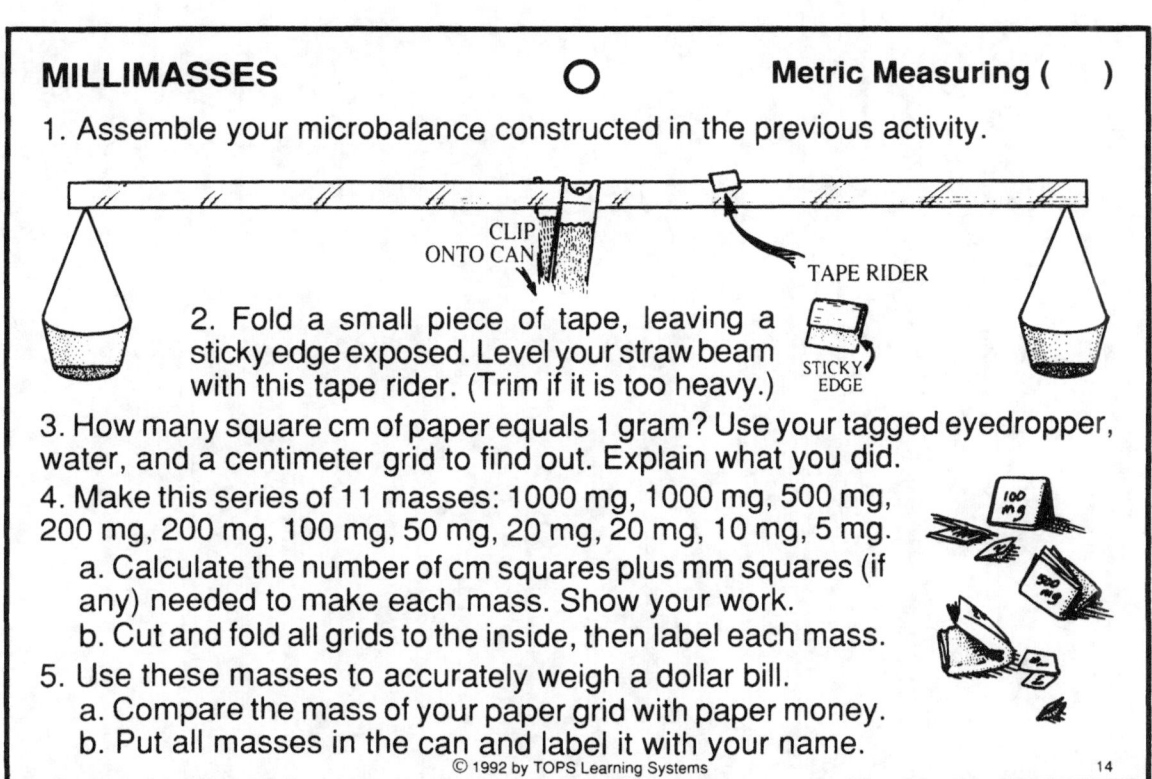

2. Fold a small piece of tape, leaving a sticky edge exposed. Level your straw beam with this tape rider. (Trim if it is too heavy.)
3. How many square cm of paper equals 1 gram? Use your tagged eyedropper, water, and a centimeter grid to find out. Explain what you did.
4. Make this series of 11 masses: 1000 mg, 1000 mg, 500 mg, 200 mg, 200 mg, 100 mg, 50 mg, 20 mg, 20 mg, 10 mg, 5 mg.
   a. Calculate the number of cm squares plus mm squares (if any) needed to make each mass. Show your work.
   b. Cut and fold all grids to the inside, then label each mass.
5. Use these masses to accurately weigh a dollar bill.
   a. Compare the mass of your paper grid with paper money.
   b. Put all masses in the can and label it with your name.

© 1992 by TOPS Learning Systems

PASS THE RICE ◯ Metric Measuring (   )

1. Fill a small jar with rice, cover it with a lid, and shake it down. Add additional rice, as much as you can, without heaping it above the rim.

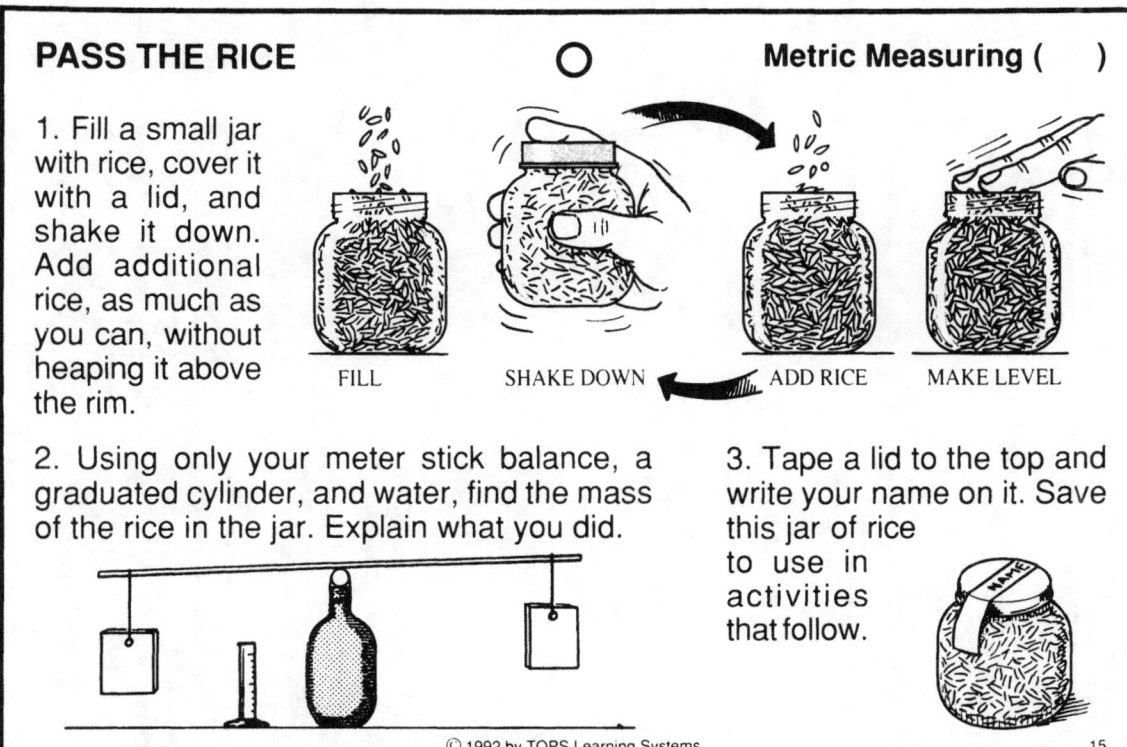

FILL — SHAKE DOWN — ADD RICE — MAKE LEVEL

2. Using only your meter stick balance, a graduated cylinder, and water, find the mass of the rice in the jar. Explain what you did.

3. Tape a lid to the top and write your name on it. Save this jar of rice to use in activities that follow.

© 1992 by TOPS Learning Systems

MASS ESTIMATE ◯ Metric Measuring (   )

1. Center your microbalance. Use it to find the total number of rice grains in 2,000 mg. (Piece together broken grains to equal whole grains).

FIND THE MASS FIRST... ...THEN COUNT IN GROUPS OF 10.

HELPFUL HINT: LEAVE YOUR RICE GROUPED FOR STEP 3!

2. Use your result to estimate the total number of grains in your whole jar. Show your math.

3. Find the mass of exactly 100 rice grains and repeat your estimate. Show your math.

4. Find the difference between your two estimates.

© 1992 by TOPS Learning Systems

VOLUME ESTIMATE   ⓞ   Metric Measuring (   )

1. Put exactly 100 grains of rice into a *dry* 10 ml graduate. Hold the base firmly while tapping the side, to settle the rice as low as possible. Estimate its average volume. **HINT:** Reserve your 100 grains.

2. Measure the volume (to the rim) of your rice storage jar with a 100 ml graduate. (Set the rice aside temporarily, then dry the jar before you pour it back.

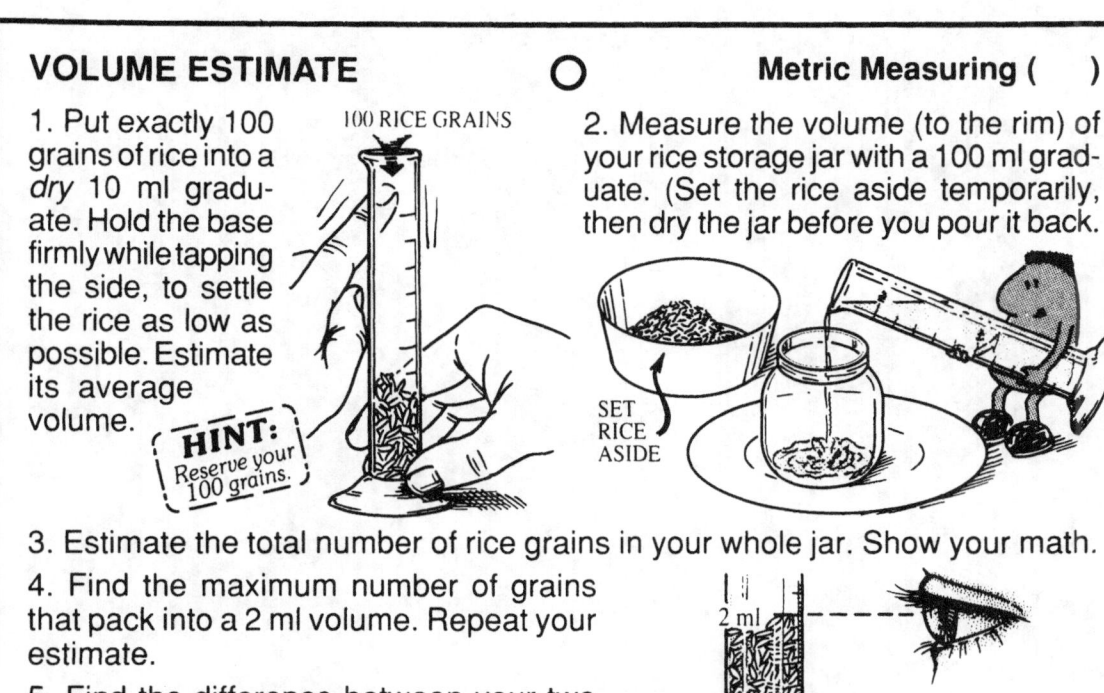

3. Estimate the total number of rice grains in your whole jar. Show your math.

4. Find the maximum number of grains that pack into a 2 ml volume. Repeat your estimate.

5. Find the difference between your two estimates.

© 1992 by TOPS Learning Systems

AREA ESTIMATE   ⓞ   Metric Measuring (   )

1. Spread all the rice in your jar across a centimeter grid. Use an index card to keep it all within the boundaries of the grid and to spread it as evenly as possible.

2. Select an average depth somewhere on your grid. Gently clear away the rice on all sides of a particular square with your pencil and count what remains. Do this in several places to decide how many rice grains an average square contains.

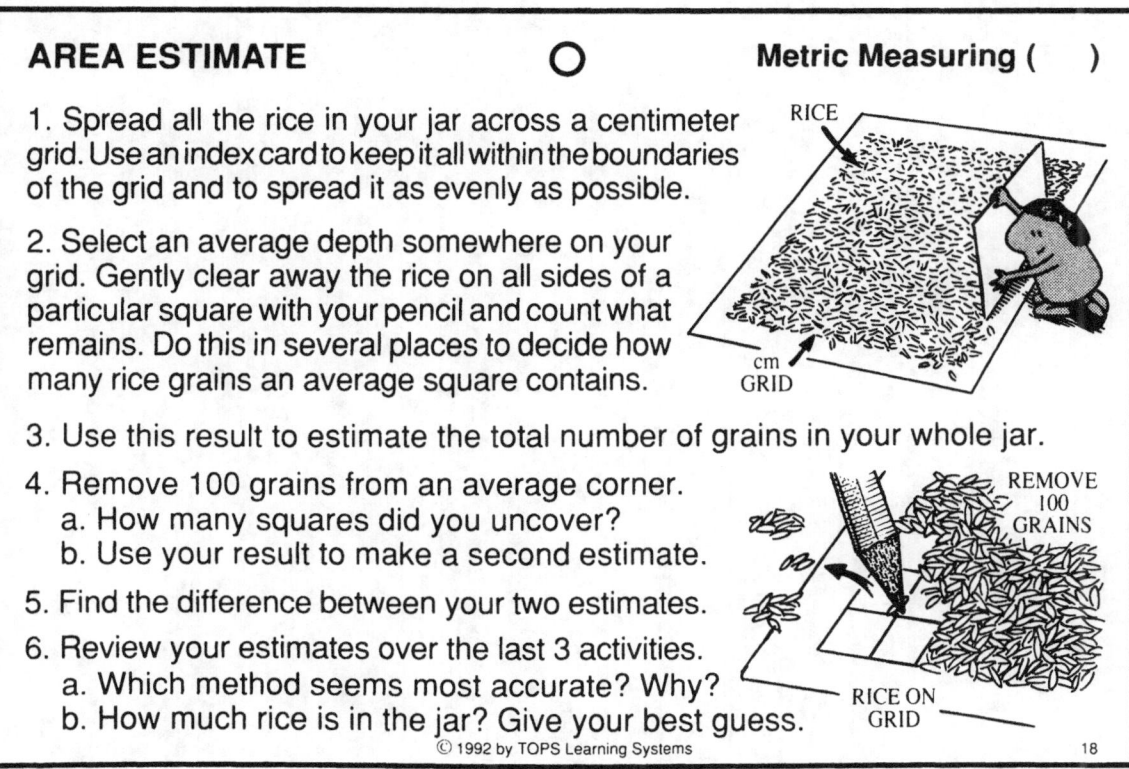

3. Use this result to estimate the total number of grains in your whole jar.

4. Remove 100 grains from an average corner.
   a. How many squares did you uncover?
   b. Use your result to make a second estimate.

5. Find the difference between your two estimates.

6. Review your estimates over the last 3 activities.
   a. Which method seems most accurate? Why?
   b. How much rice is in the jar? Give your best guess.

© 1992 by TOPS Learning Systems

cards 17-18

HOW CAN THIS BE? ○ Metric Measuring (   )

1. Draw *two* triangles and *two* trapezoids on a centimeter grid like these. Cut them out.

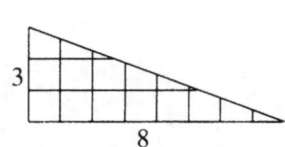 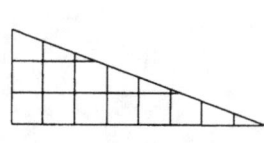 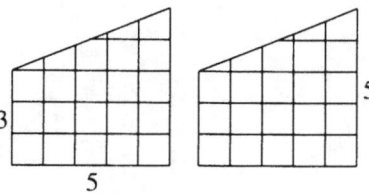

2. Put the four pieces together to form an 8 x 8 cm square.
   a. Sketch your solution.
   b. What is the area of this square?

3. Rearrange the four pieces to from a 5 x 13 cm rectangle. (You'll need to turn two of the pieces over.)
   a. Sketch your solution.
   b. What is the area of this rectangle?

4. Identical puzzle pieces assemble into two shapes with different areas! How can this be?

© 1992 by TOPS Learning Systems   19

A TON OF WATER ○ Metric Measuring (   )

1. Draw a 10 cm cube pattern on newspaper. Use your 10 cm square as a template.

2. Cut and tape it into an open cube. What is the liquid volume of this cube?

3. Make a faucet slowly drip water. How many total drops would fill your model (if it didn't leak)?

4. Assume your faucet drips one drop per second. How long would it take to fill your cube?

5. How long would it take your dripping faucet to fill a whole cubic meter?

6. A metric ton equals 1,000 kg. If you failed to fix your dripping faucet, how much time would pass before you wasted a ton of water?

© 1992 by TOPS Learning Systems   20

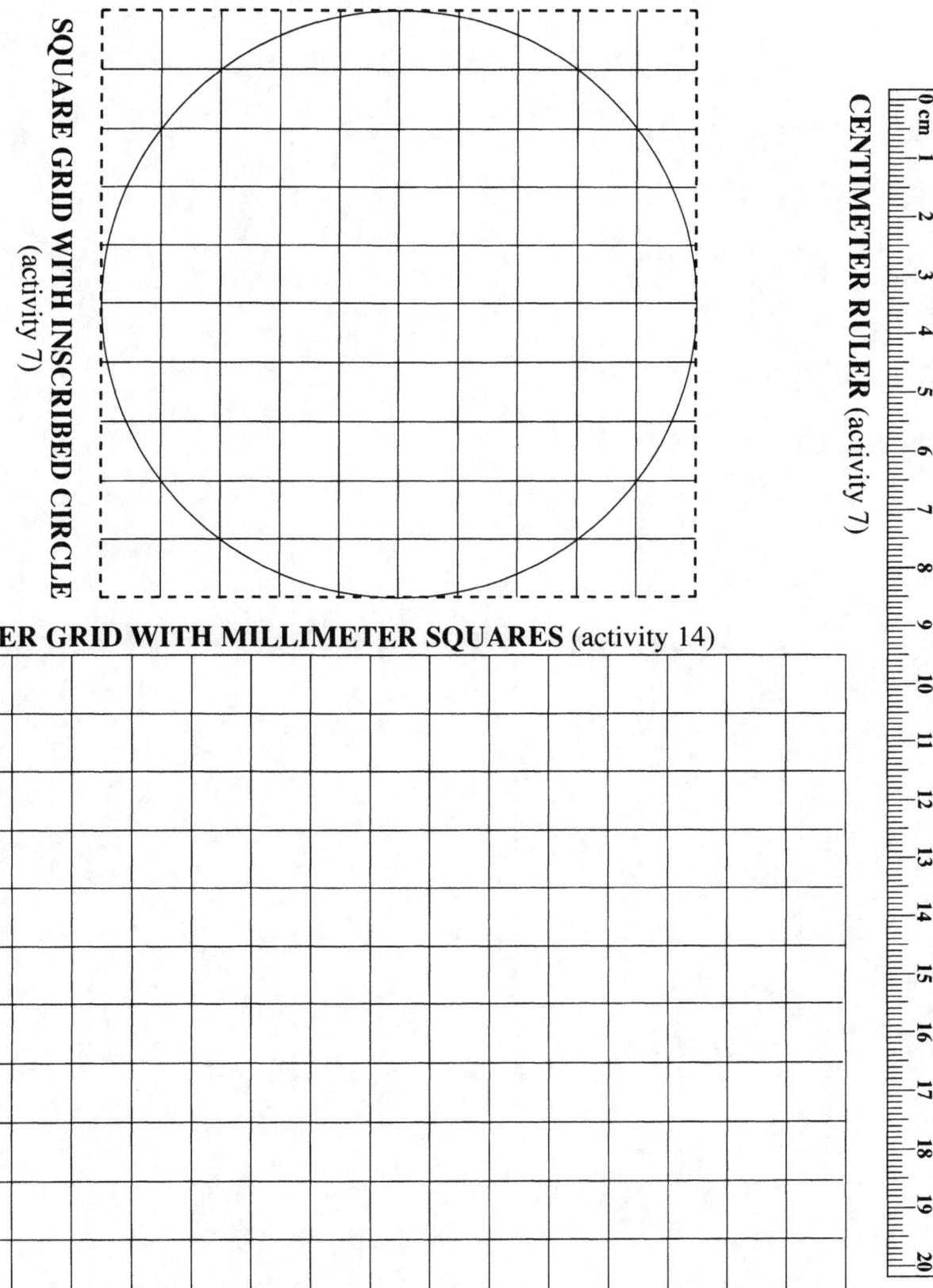

CENTIMETER GRID

Feedback

If you enjoyed teaching TOPS please tell us so. Your praise motivates us to work hard. If you found an error or can suggest ways to improve this module, we need to hear about that too. Your criticism will help us improve our next new edition. Would you like information about our other publications? Ask us to send you our latest catalog free of charge.

For whatever reason, we'd love to hear from you. We include this self-mailer for your convenience.

Sincerely,

Ron and Peg Marson
author and illustrator

Your Message Here:

Module Title _____ Date _____

Name _____ School _____

Address _____

City _____ State _____ Zip _____

—————————————— FIRST FOLD ——————————————

—————————————— SECOND FOLD ——————————————

RETURN ADDRESS

_____

_____

_____

PLACE
STAMP
HERE

TOPS Learning Systems
342 S Plumas St
Willows, CA 95988

TAPE HERE

www.ingramcontent.com/pod-product-compliance
Lightning Source LLC
Chambersburg PA
CBHW080923180426

43192CB00040B/2674